KIDS & KLASSROOM

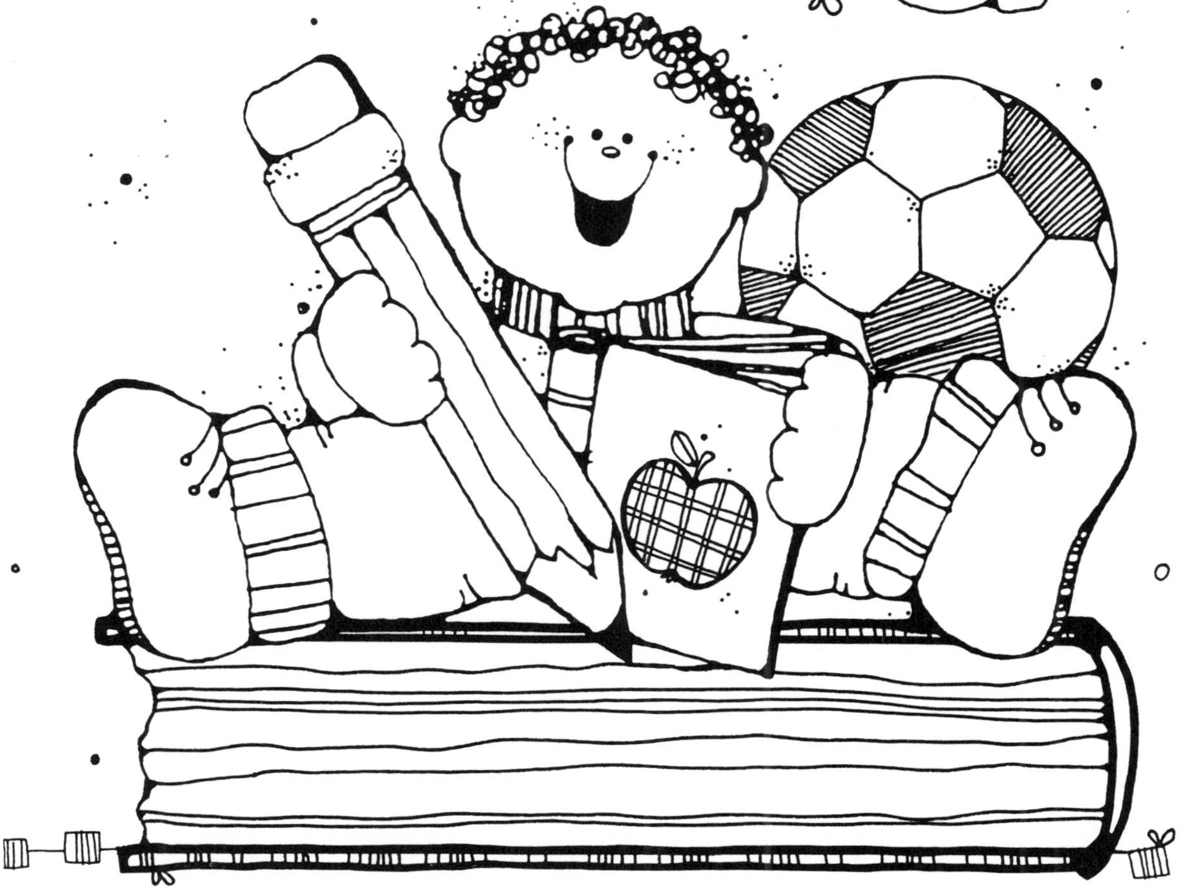

D.J. INKERS , Post Office Box 2462 / Sandy, UT 84091

Printed in the USA

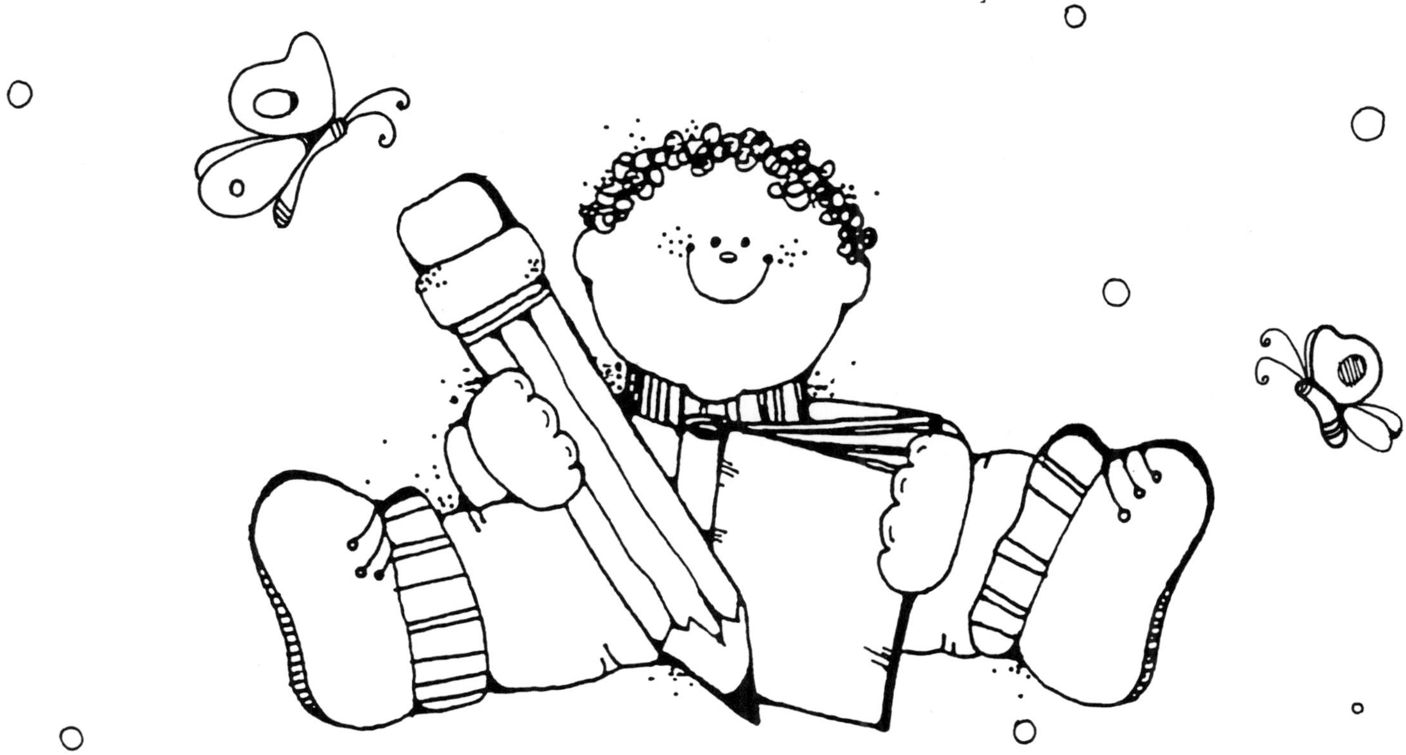

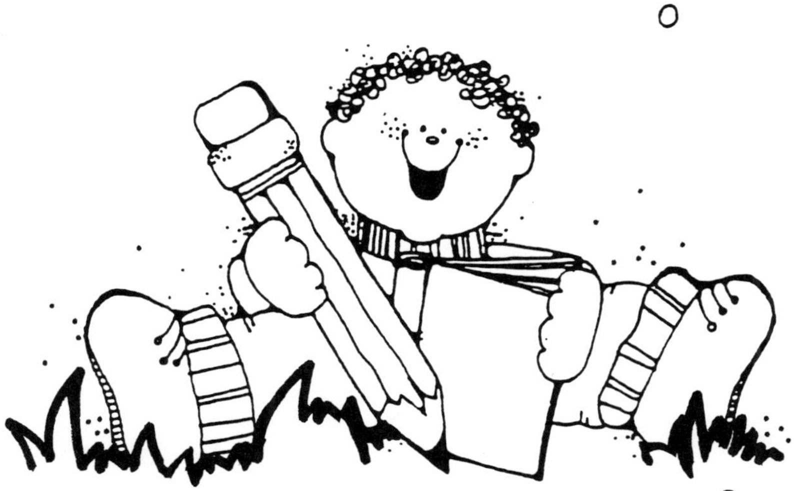

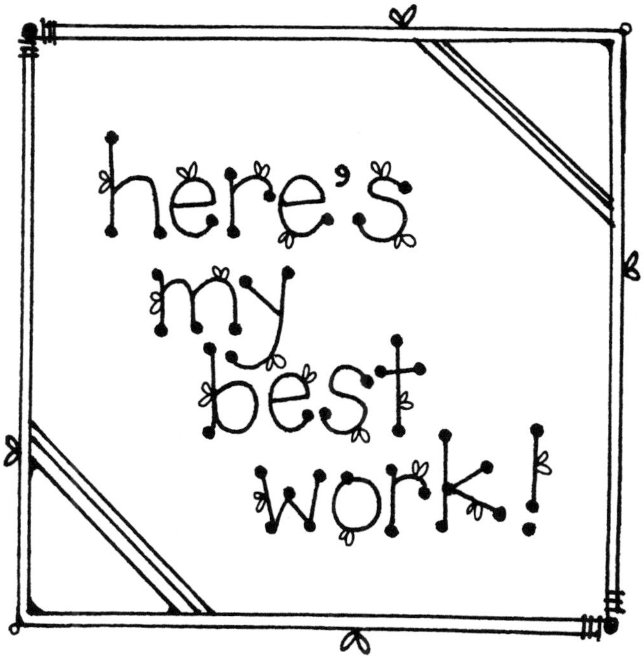
here's
my
best
work!

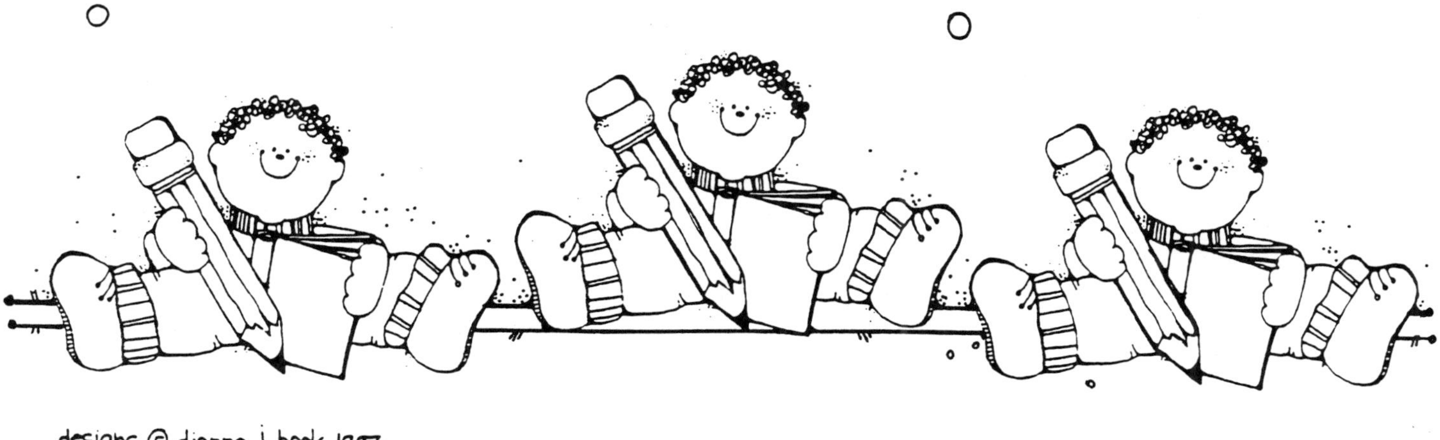

BACK TO SCHOOL

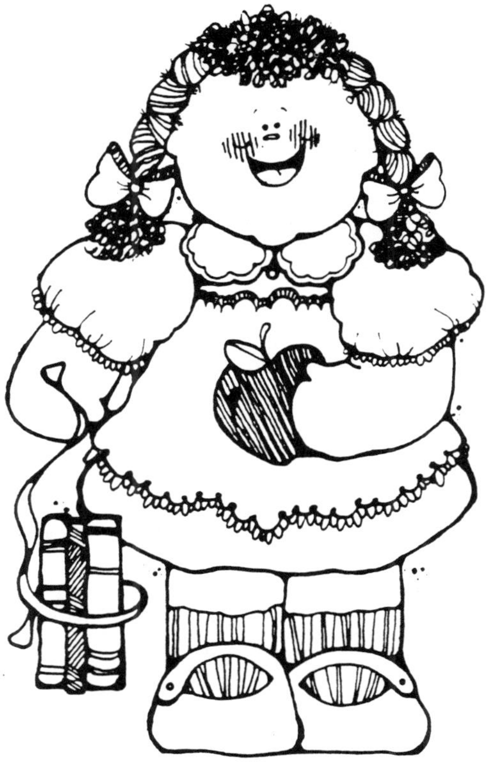

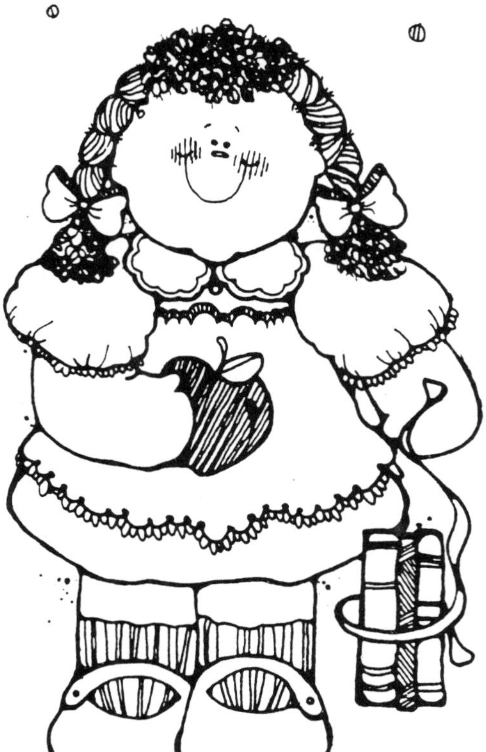

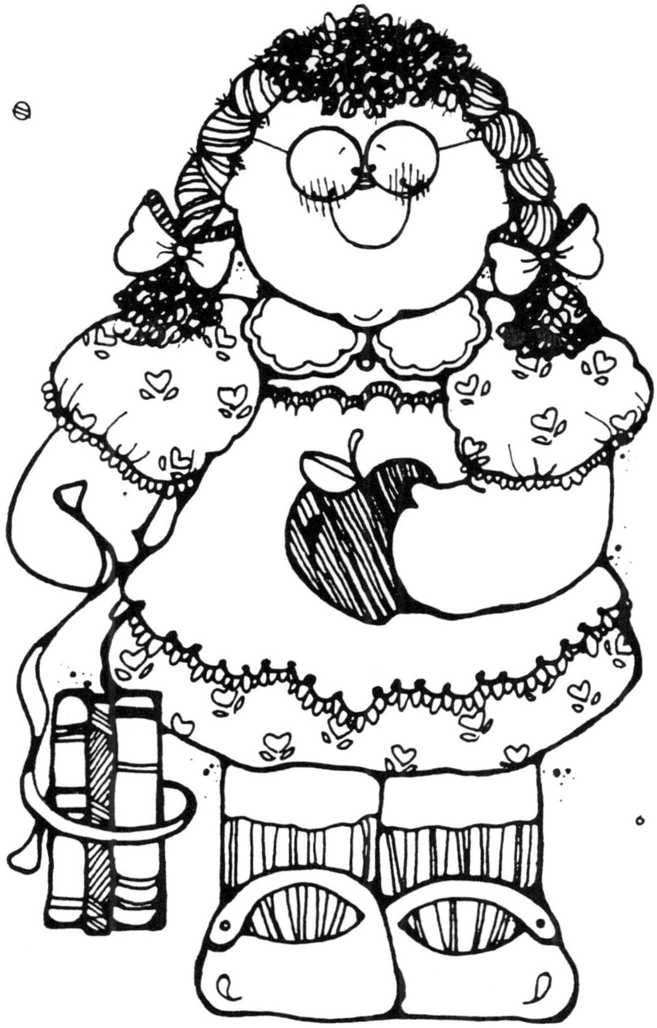

School days
school days
good ol' fashioned
rule days...

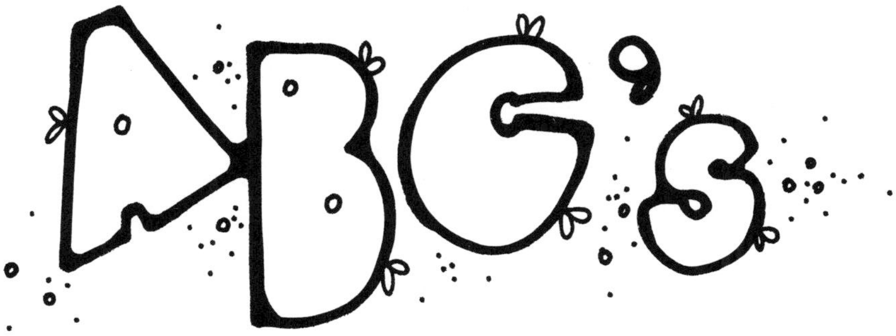
ABC's

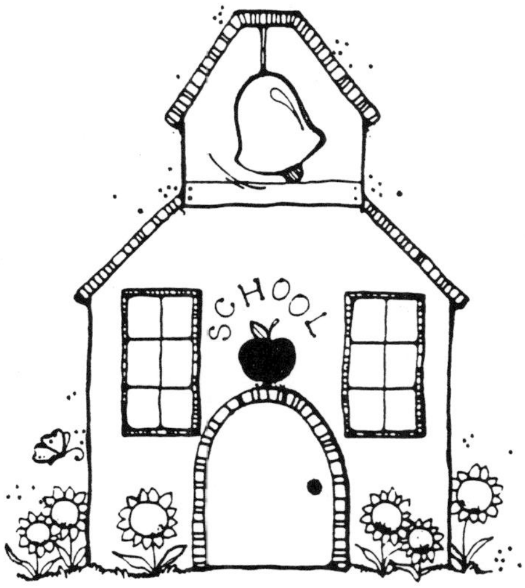
SCHOOL

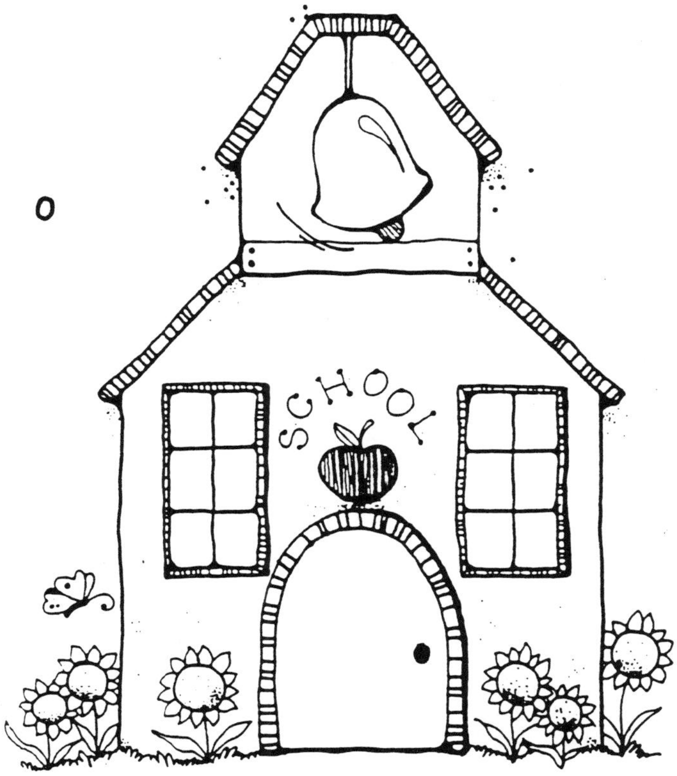
SCHOOL

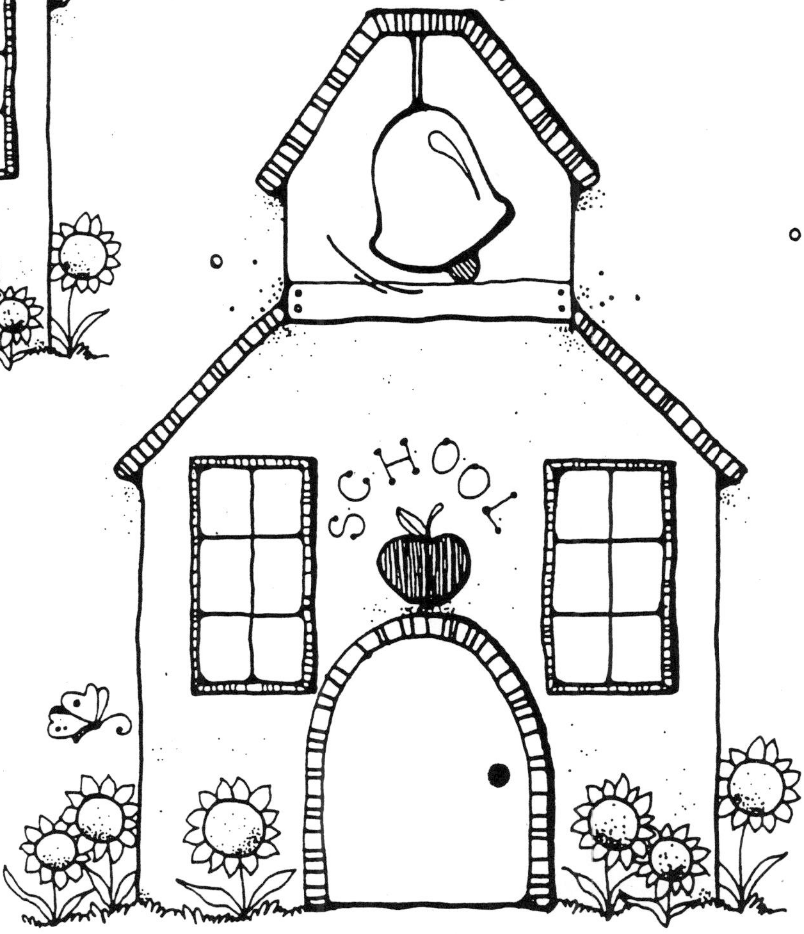
SCHOOL

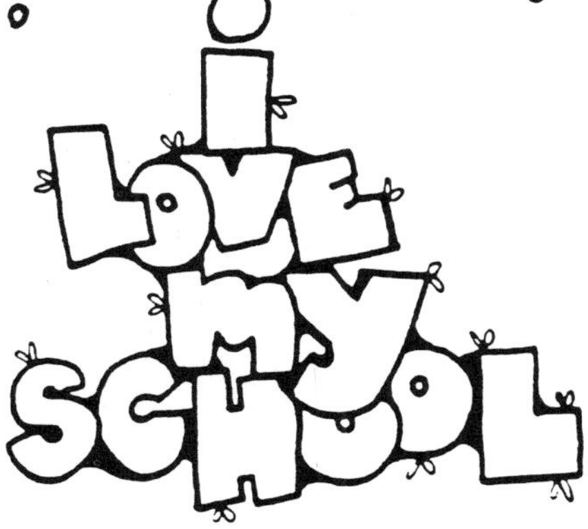
i LOVE MY SCHOOL

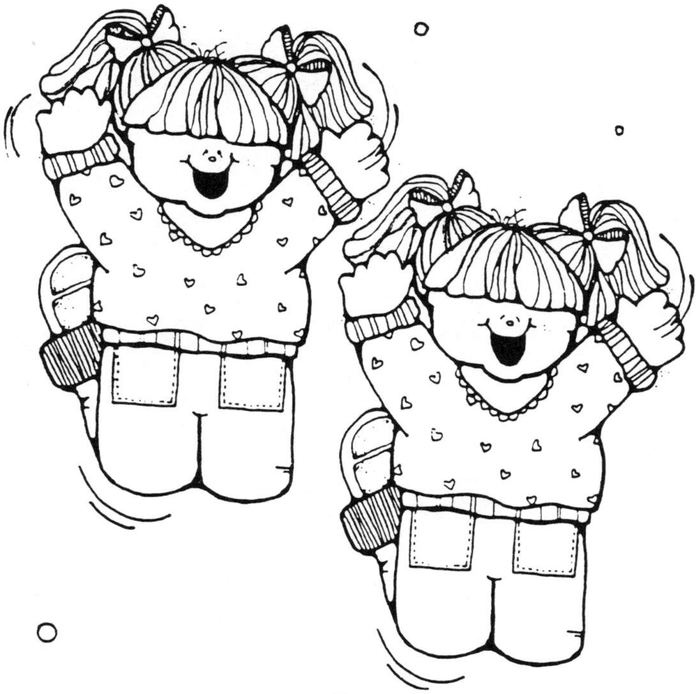

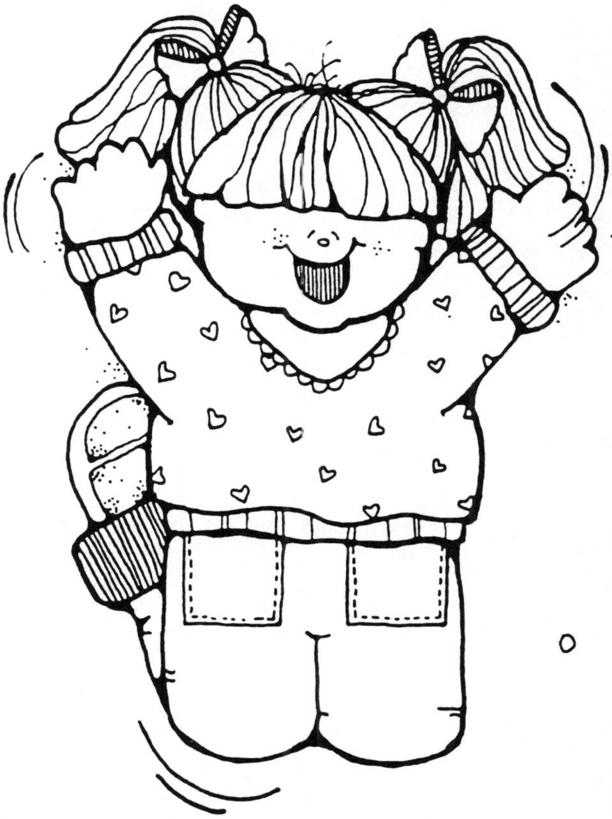

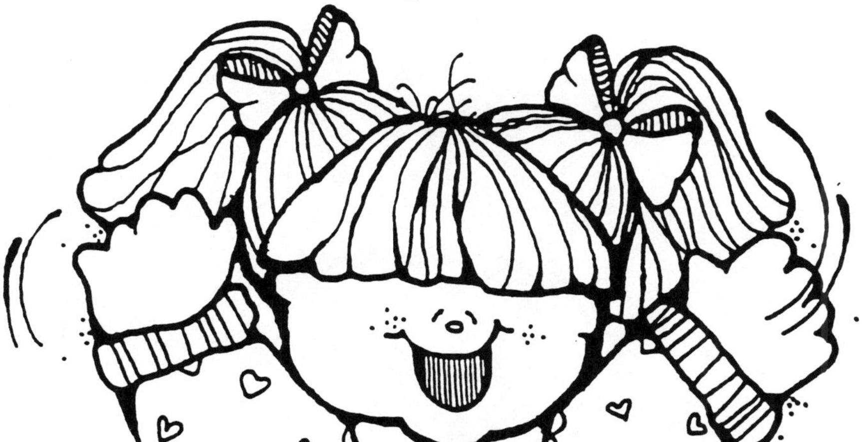

SUPER KID!

HOORAY FOR YOU!

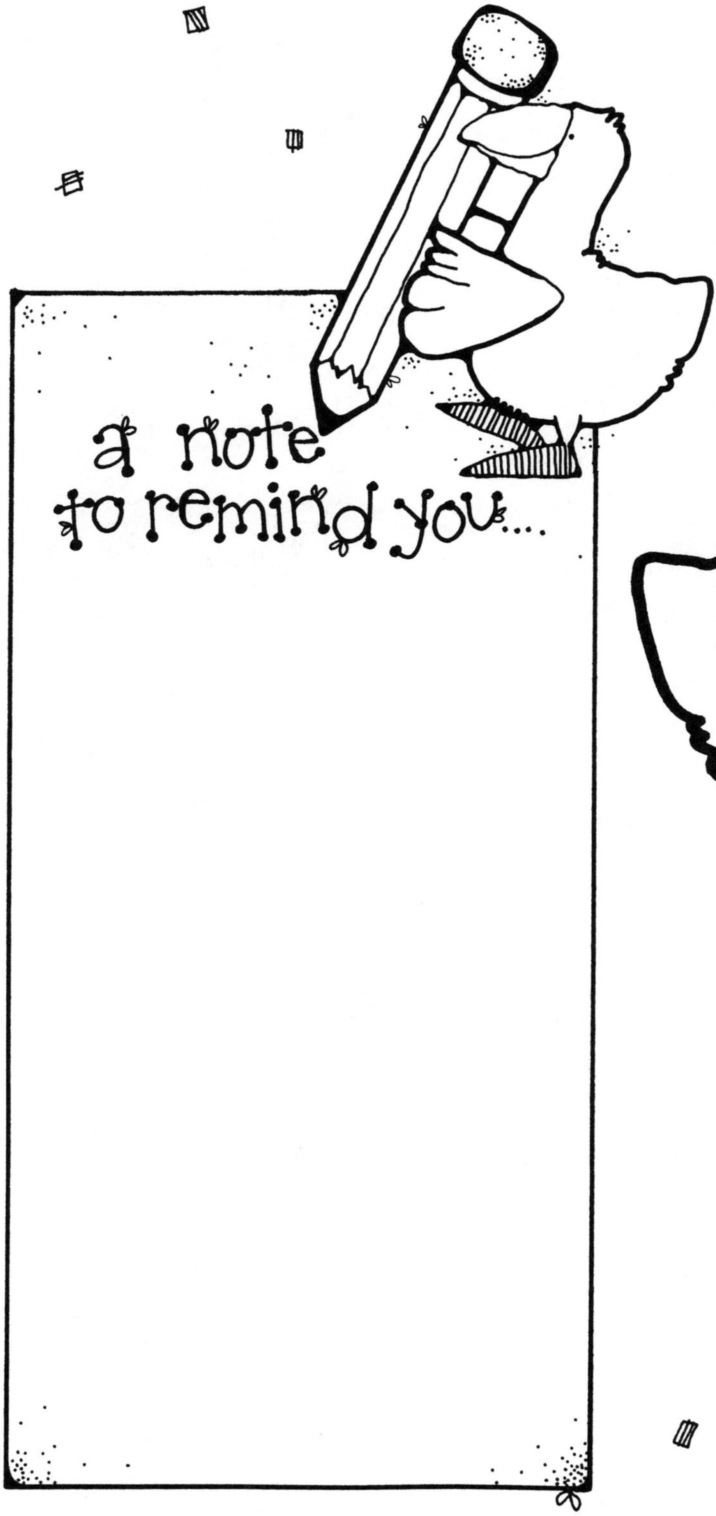
a note
to remind you...

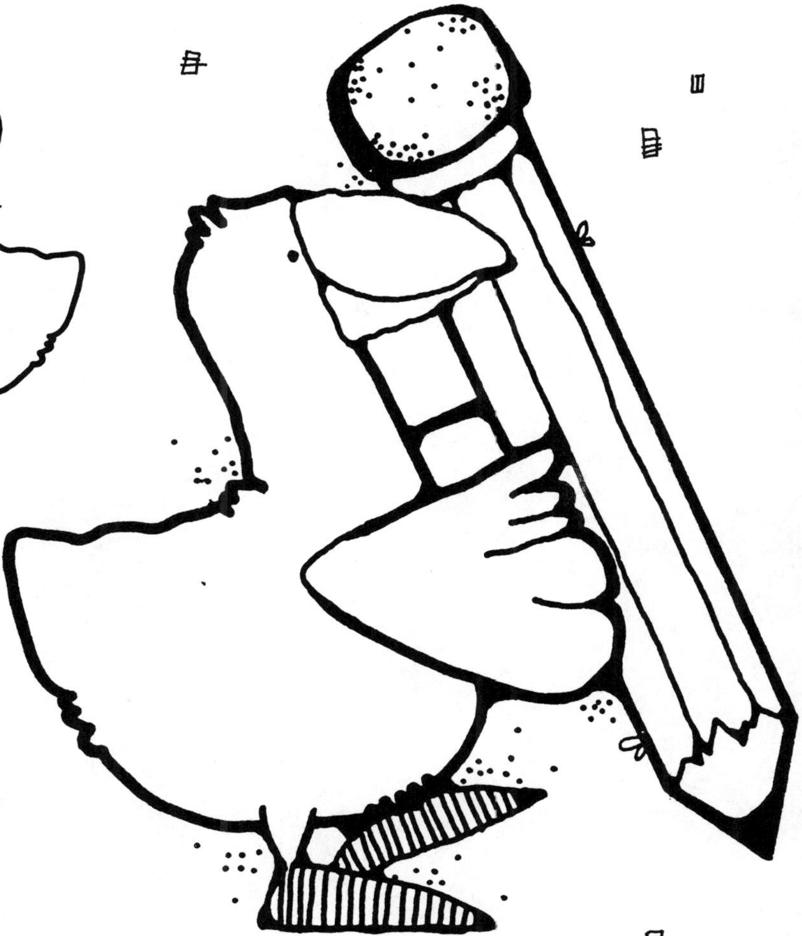

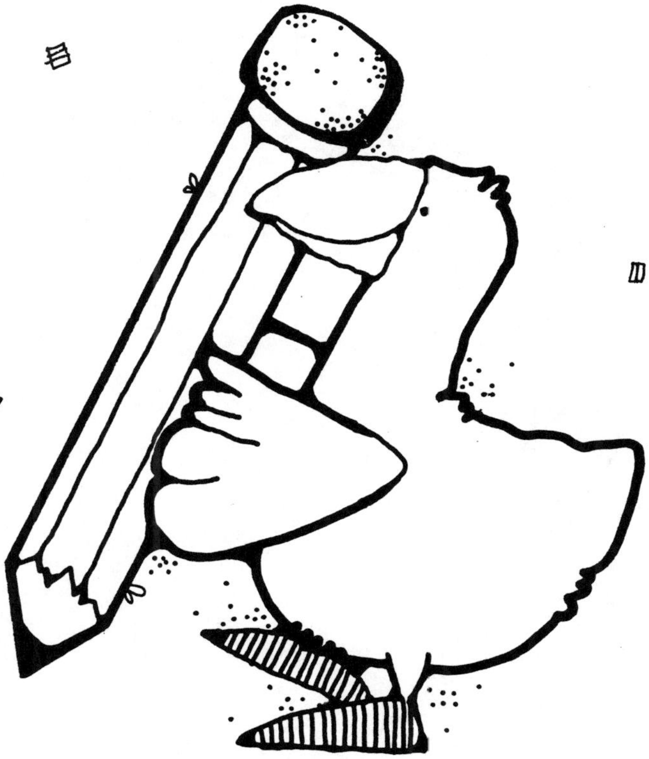

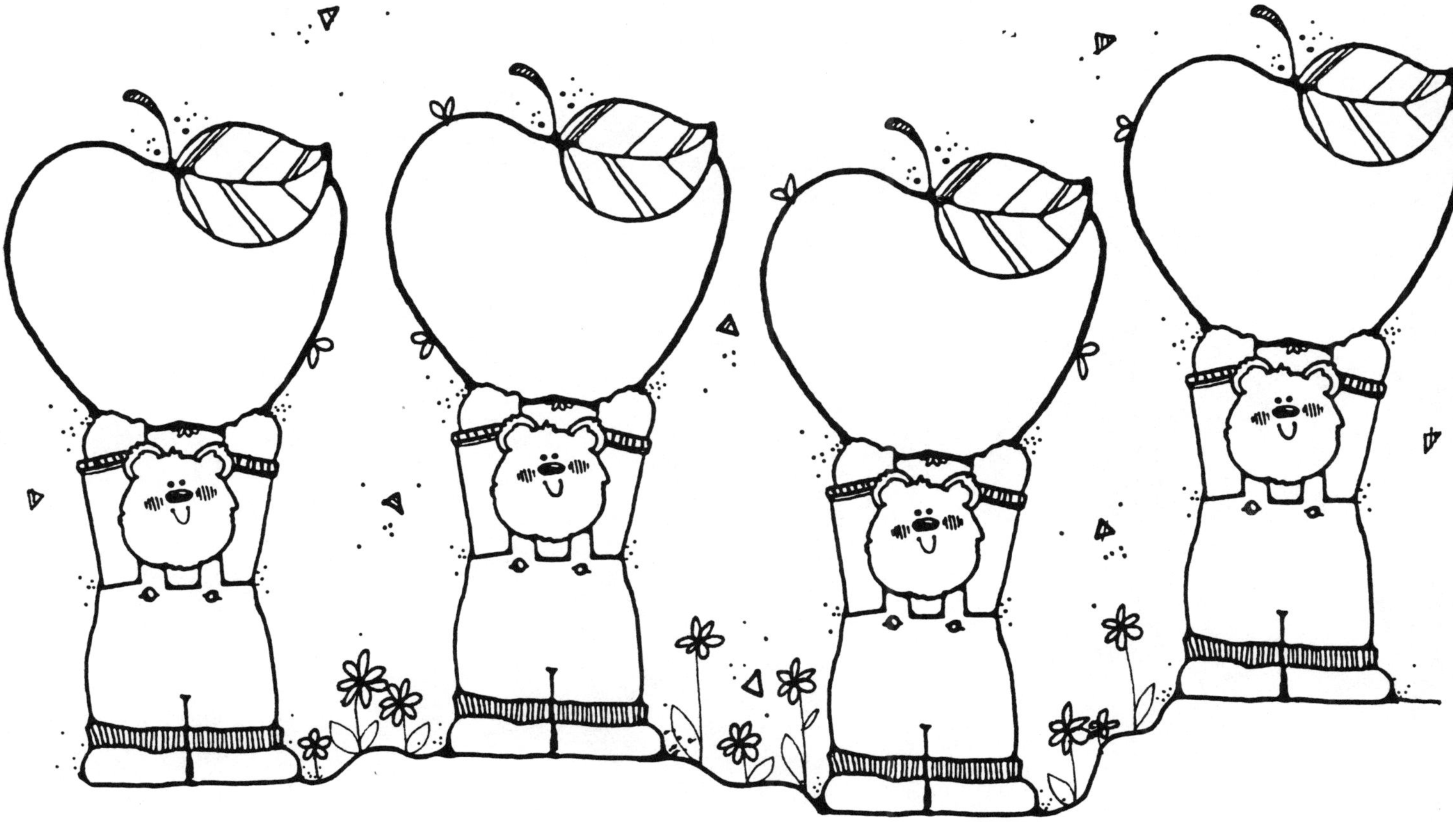

BOOK REPORT

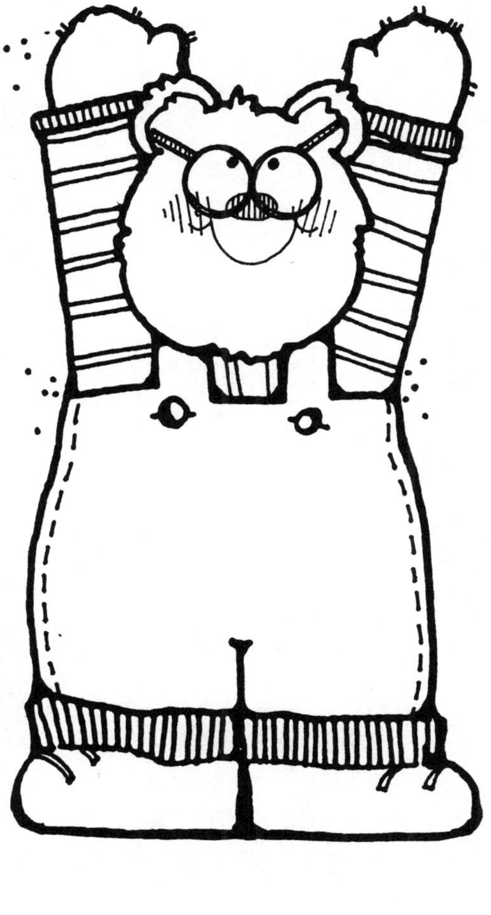

a NOTE TO PARENTS

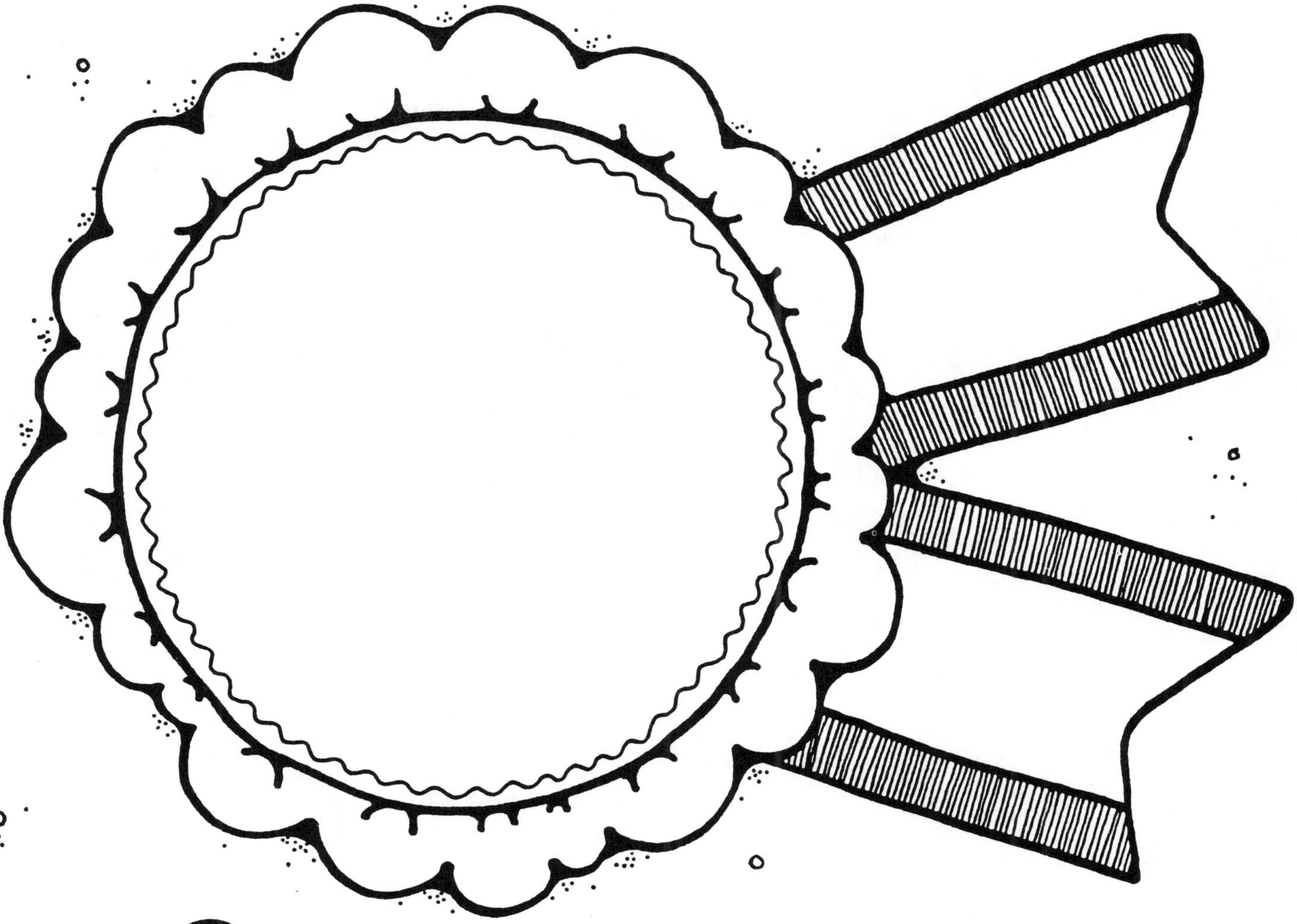

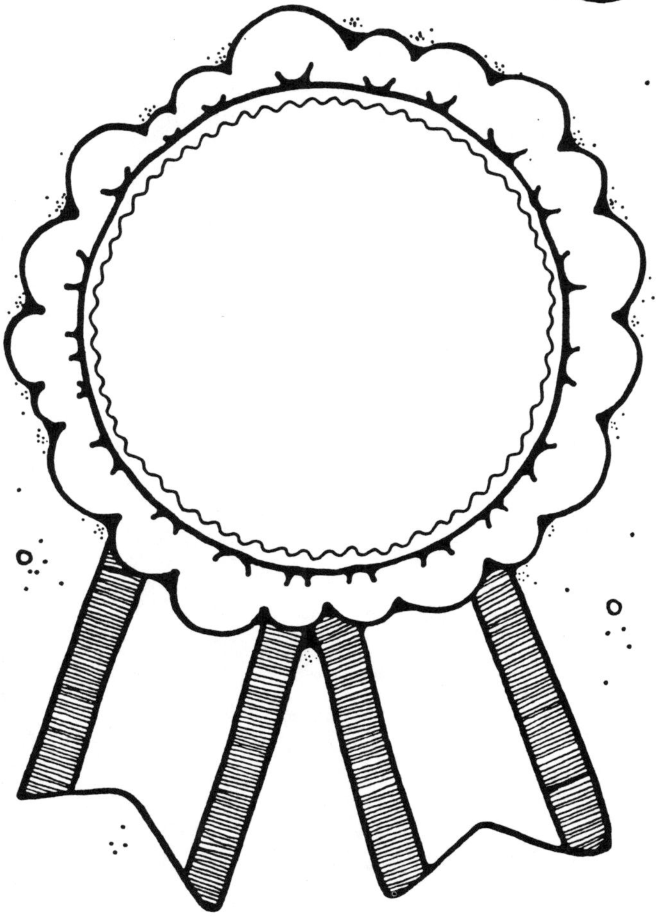

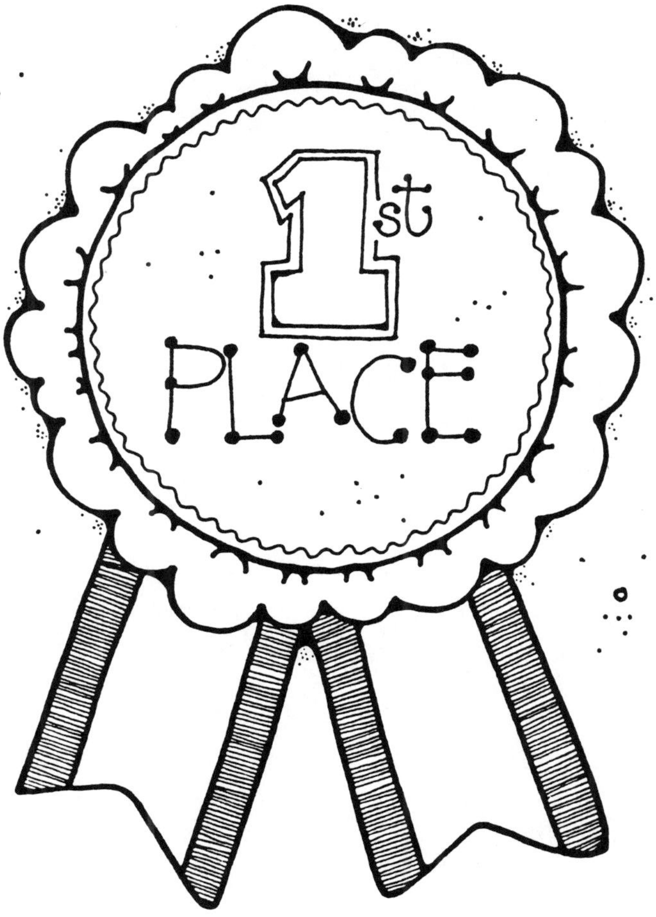
1st
PLACE

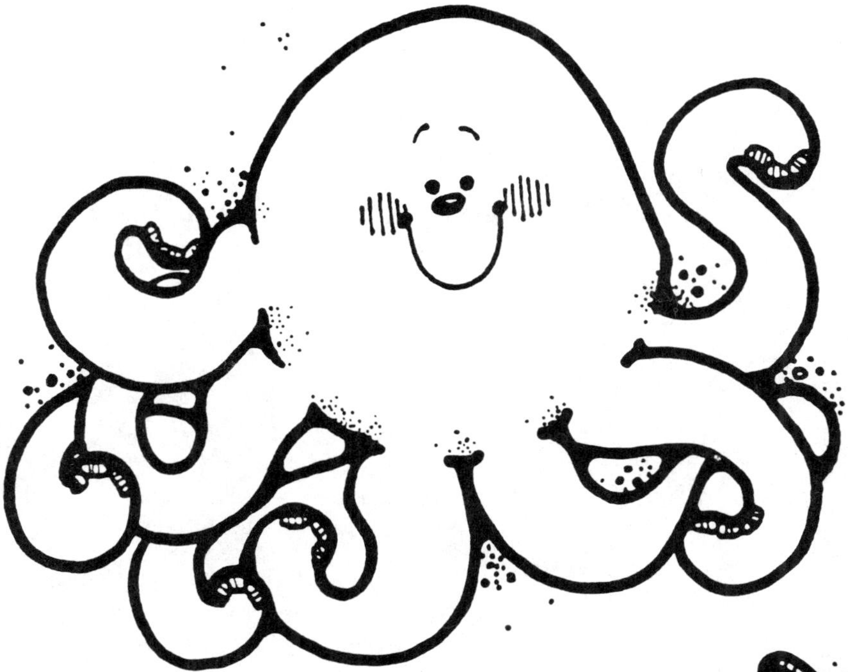

WE REALLY GOTTA' HAND IT TO YOU!

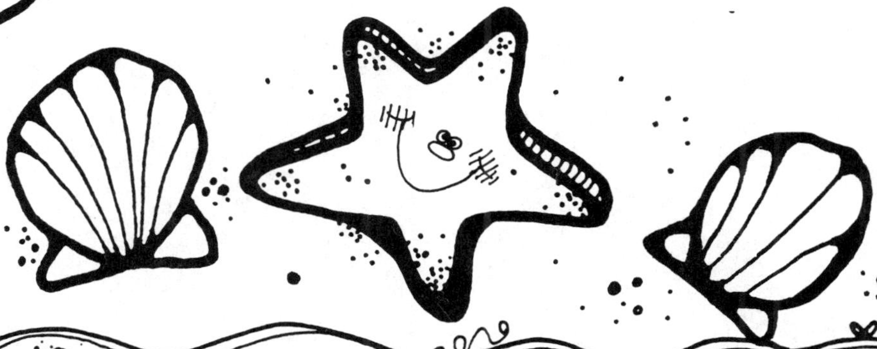

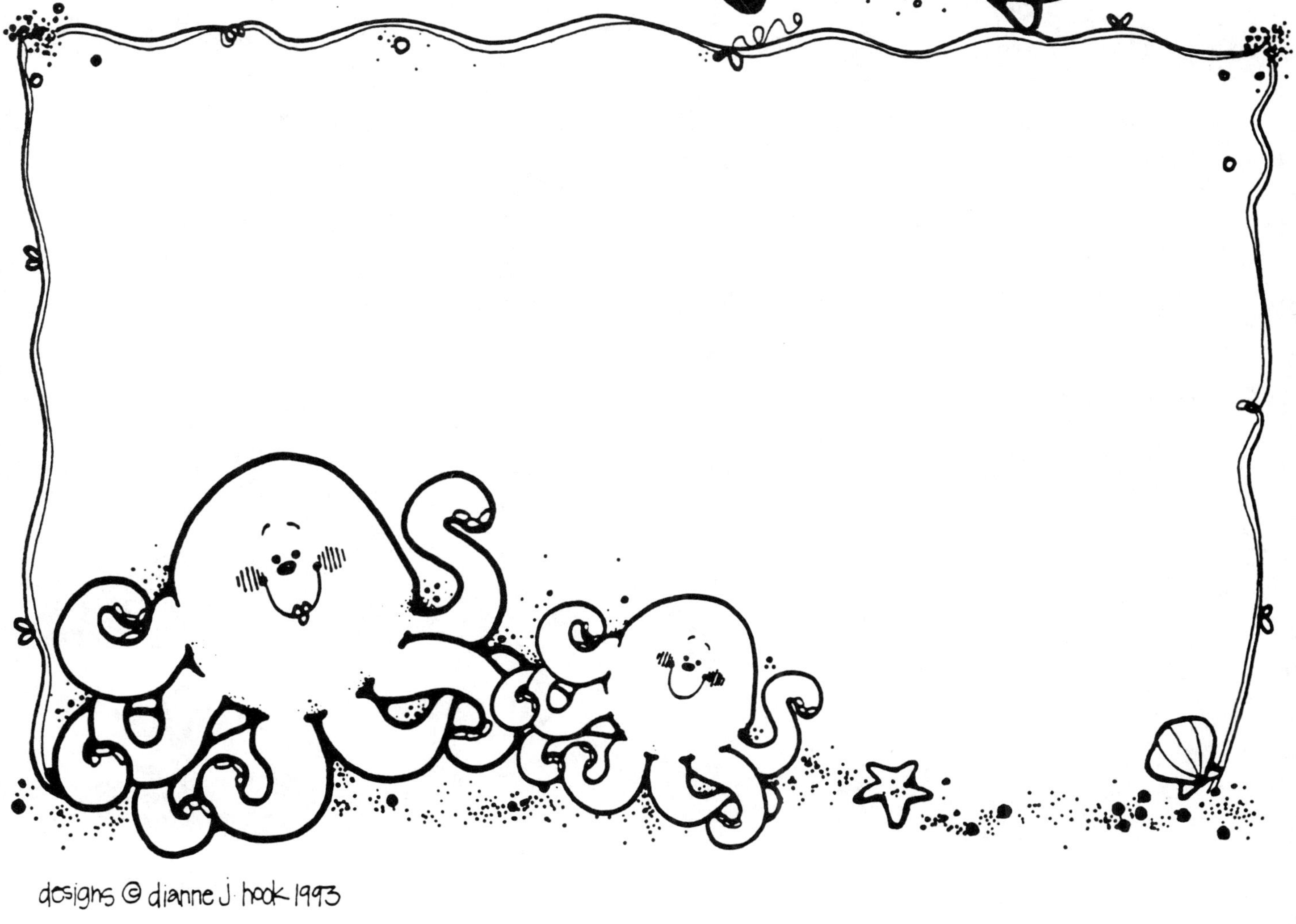

'Purr'fect Work!

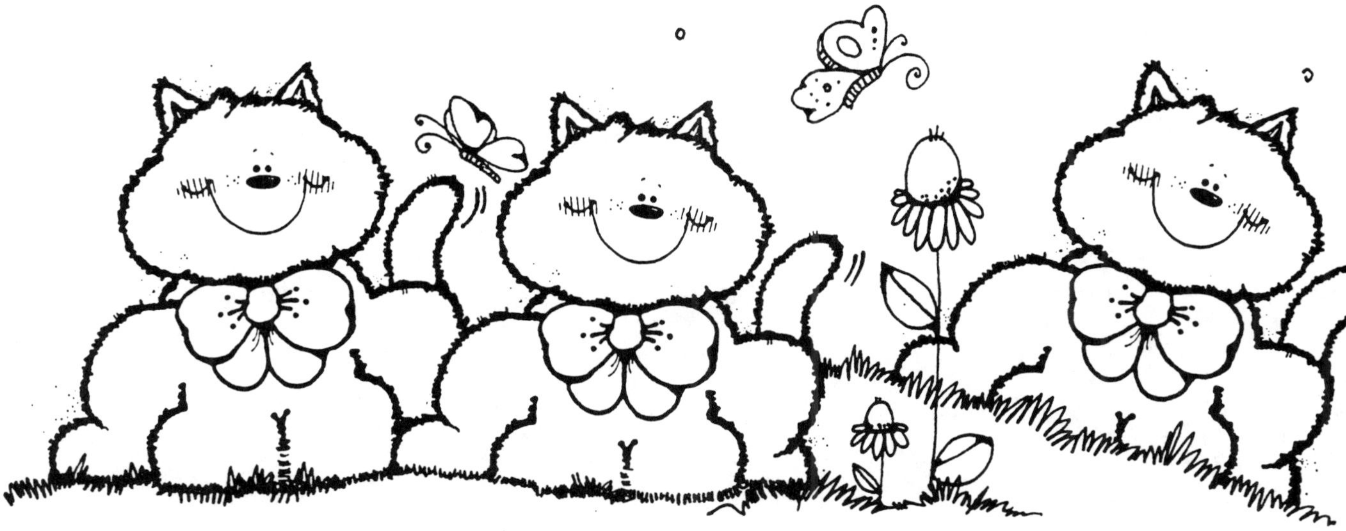

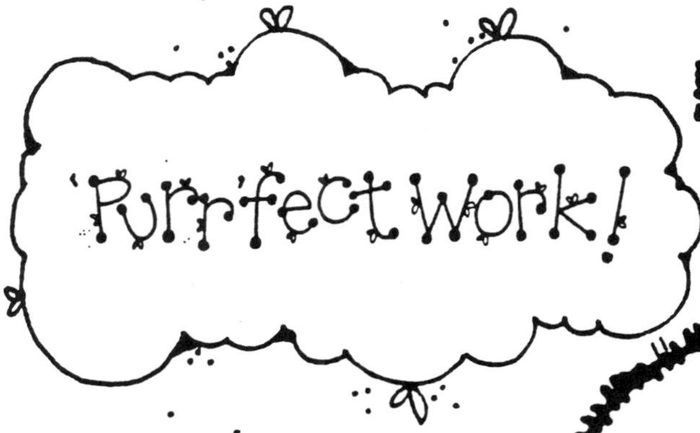

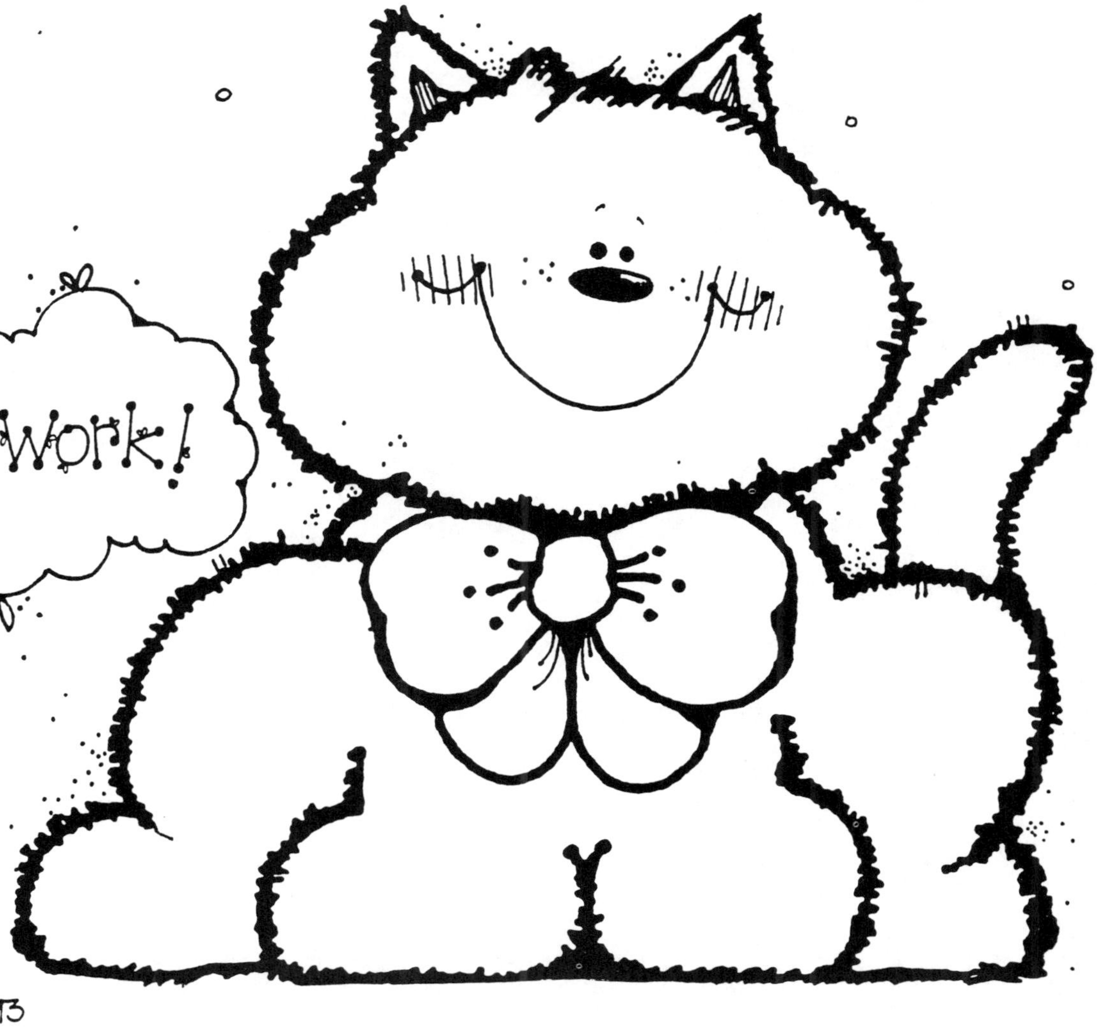

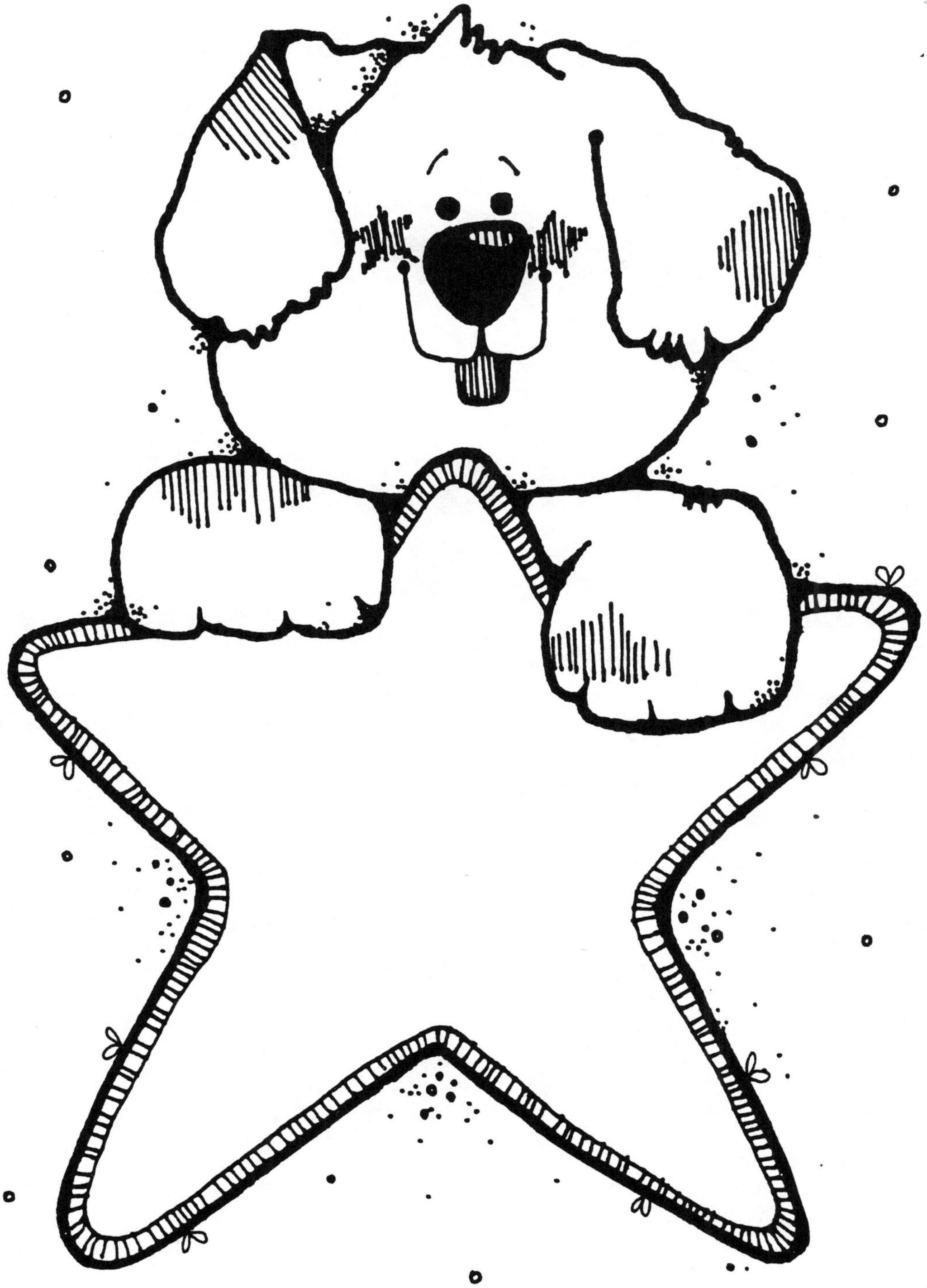

SUPER STAR!

all star class

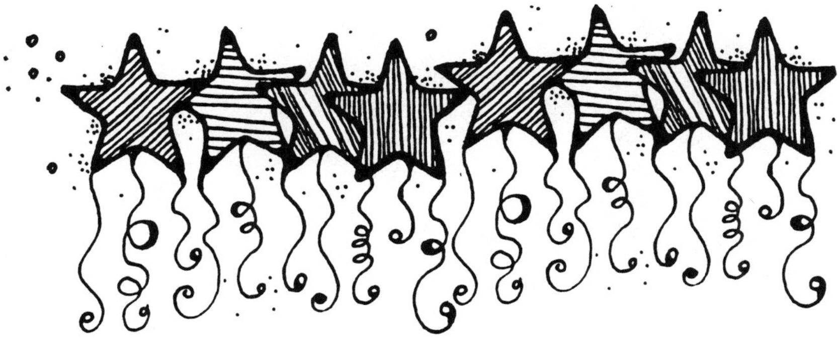

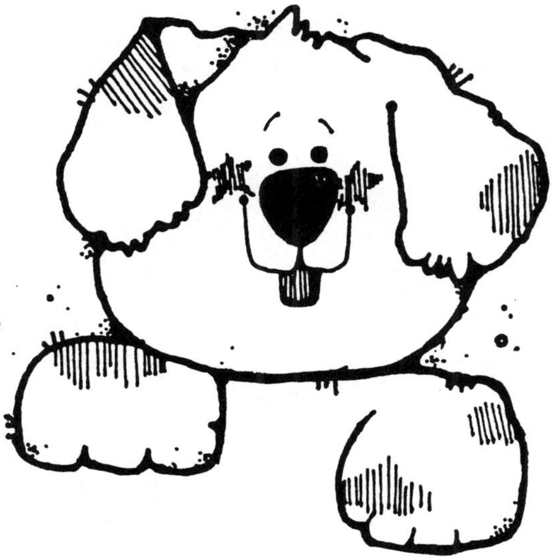

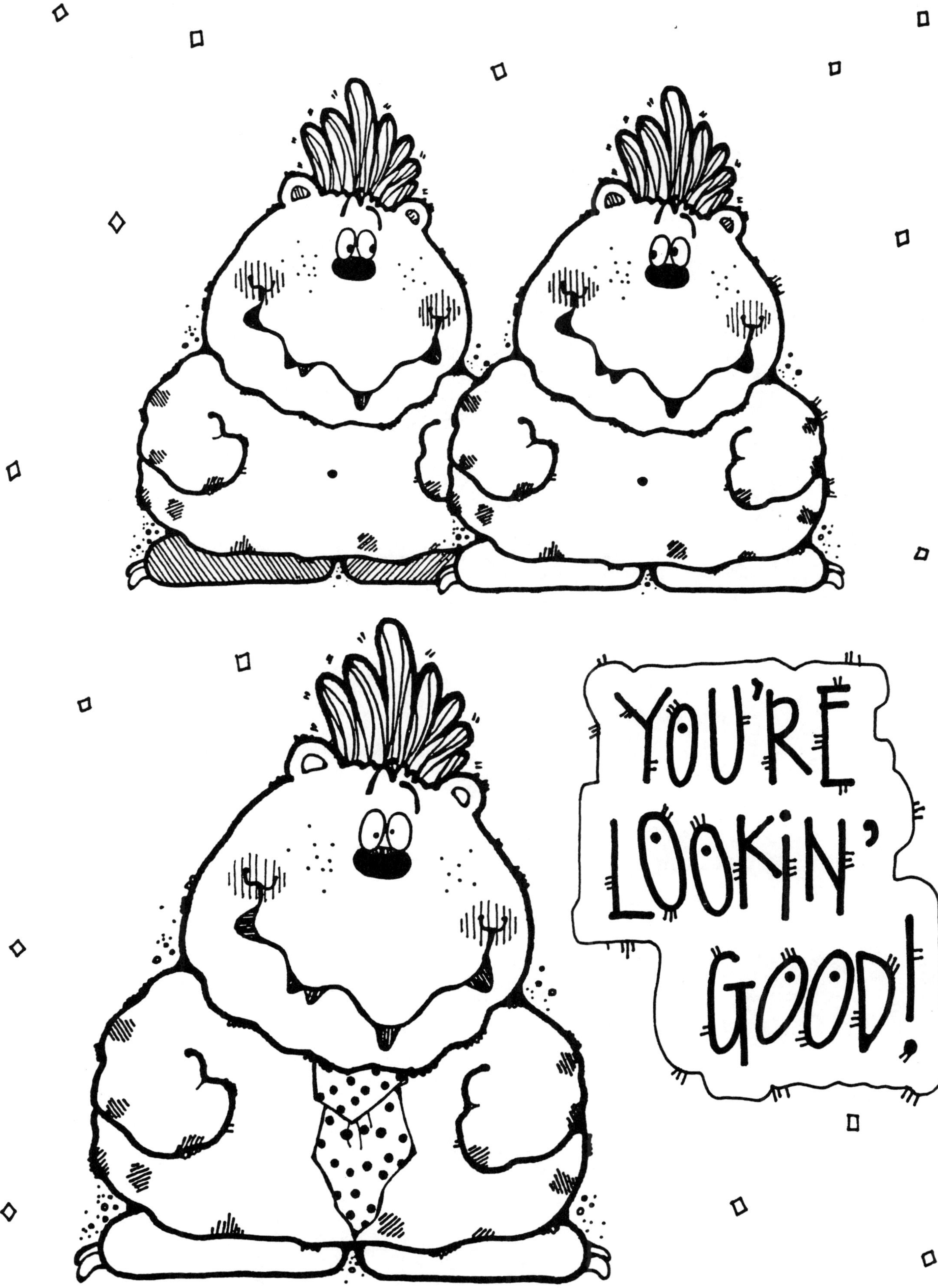
YOU'RE LOOKIN' GOOD!

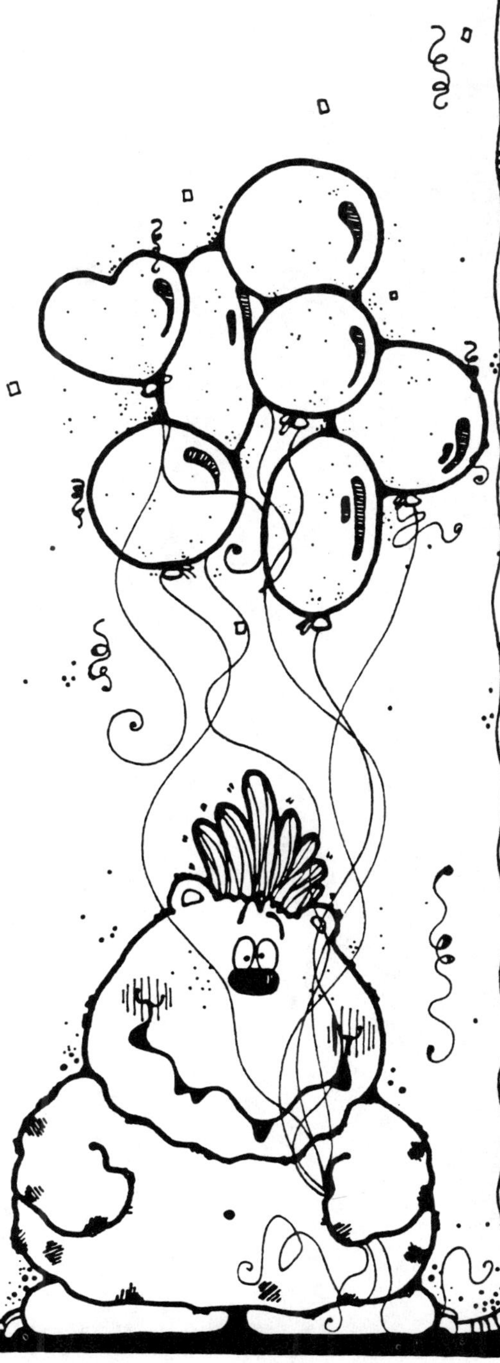

CIRCUS

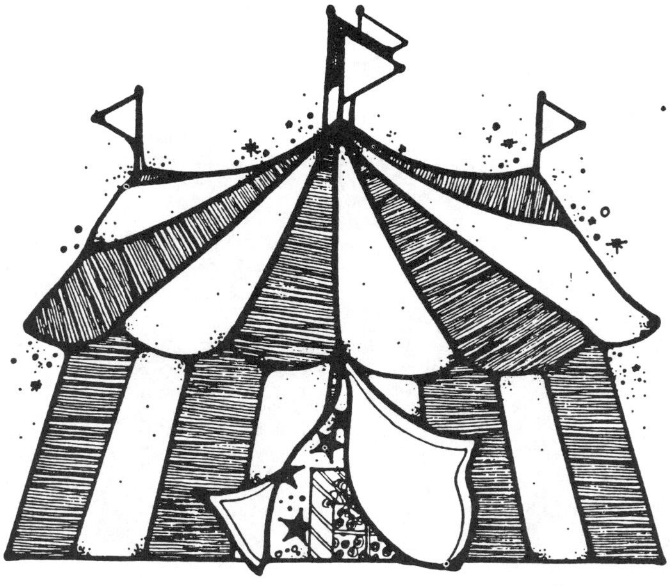

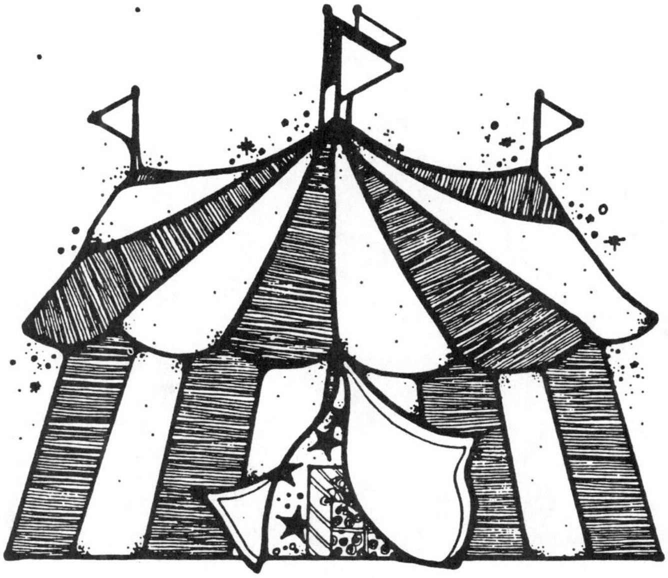

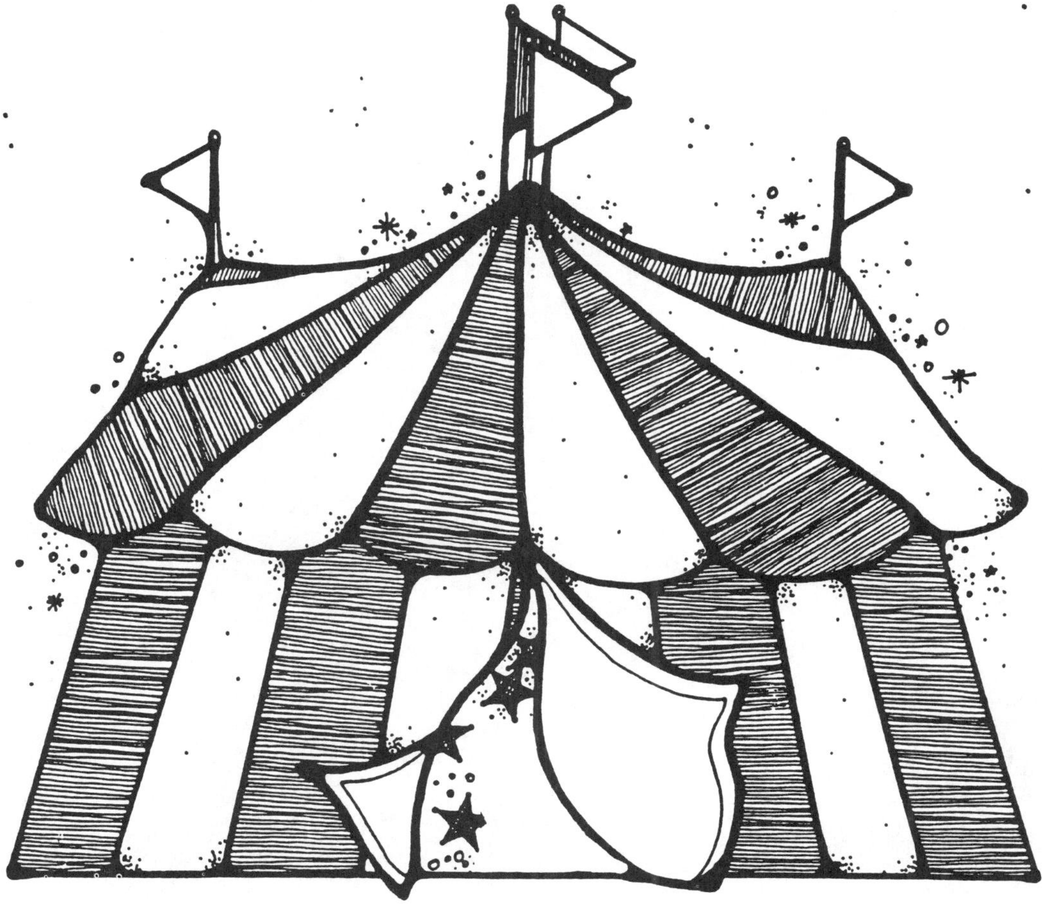

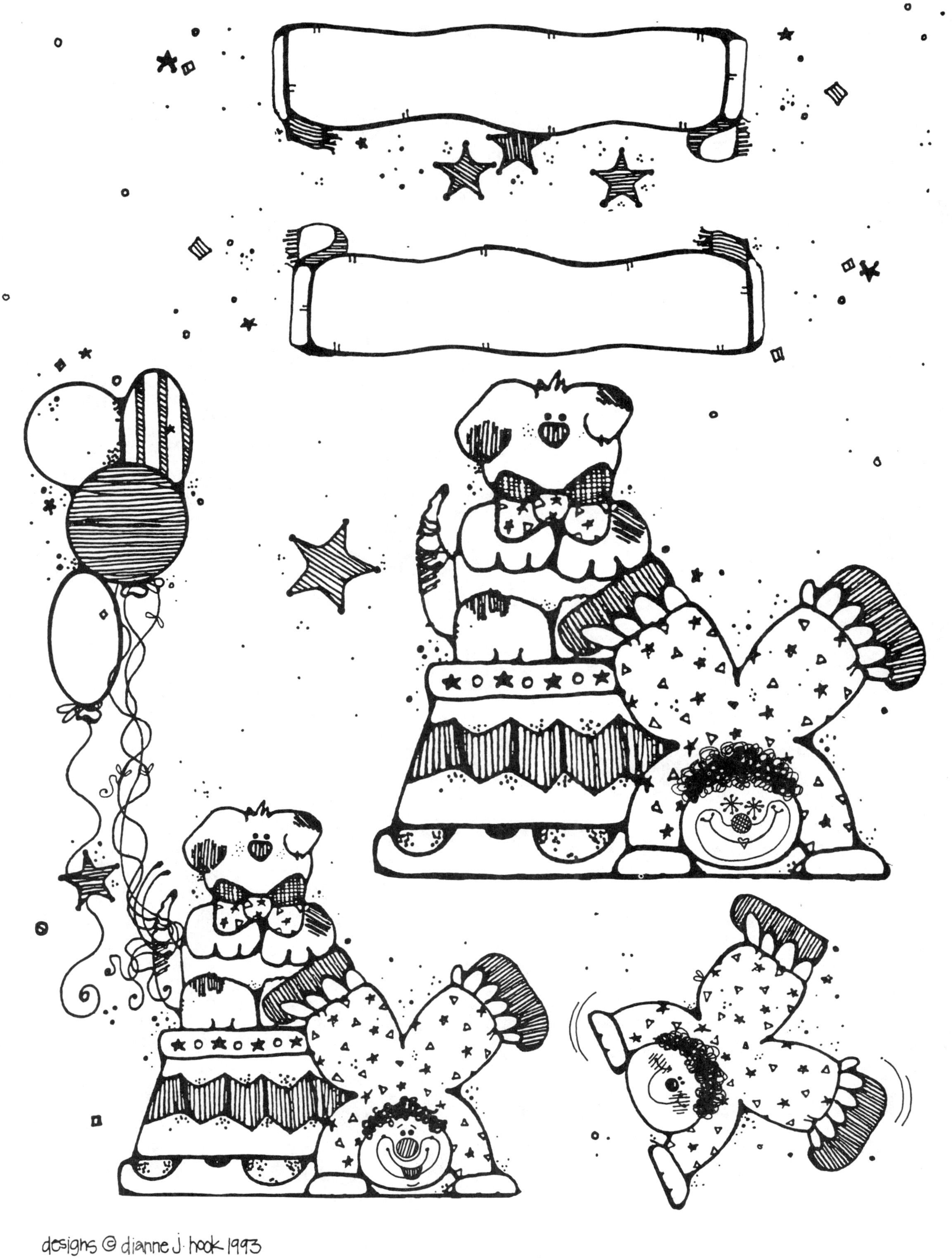

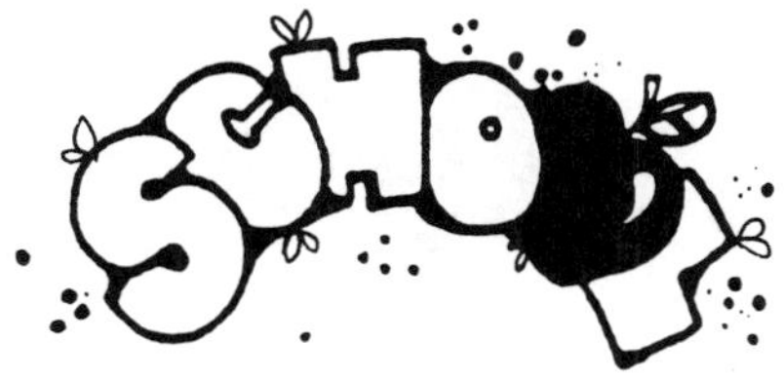

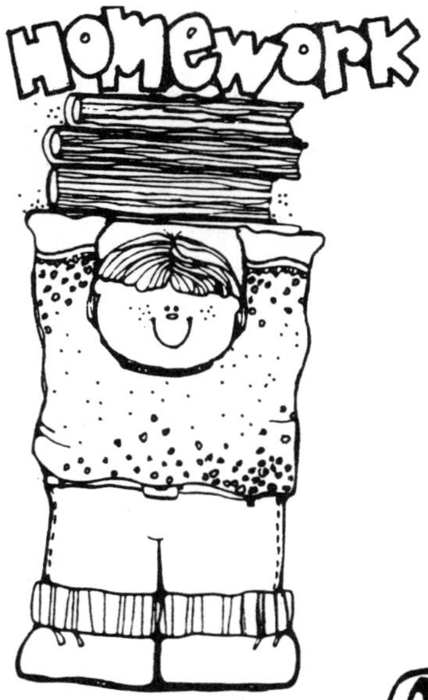
HOMEWORK

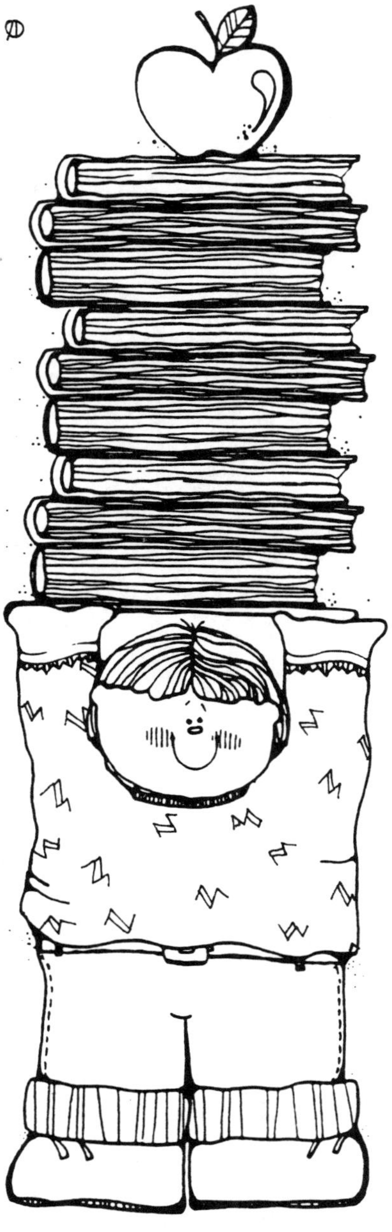

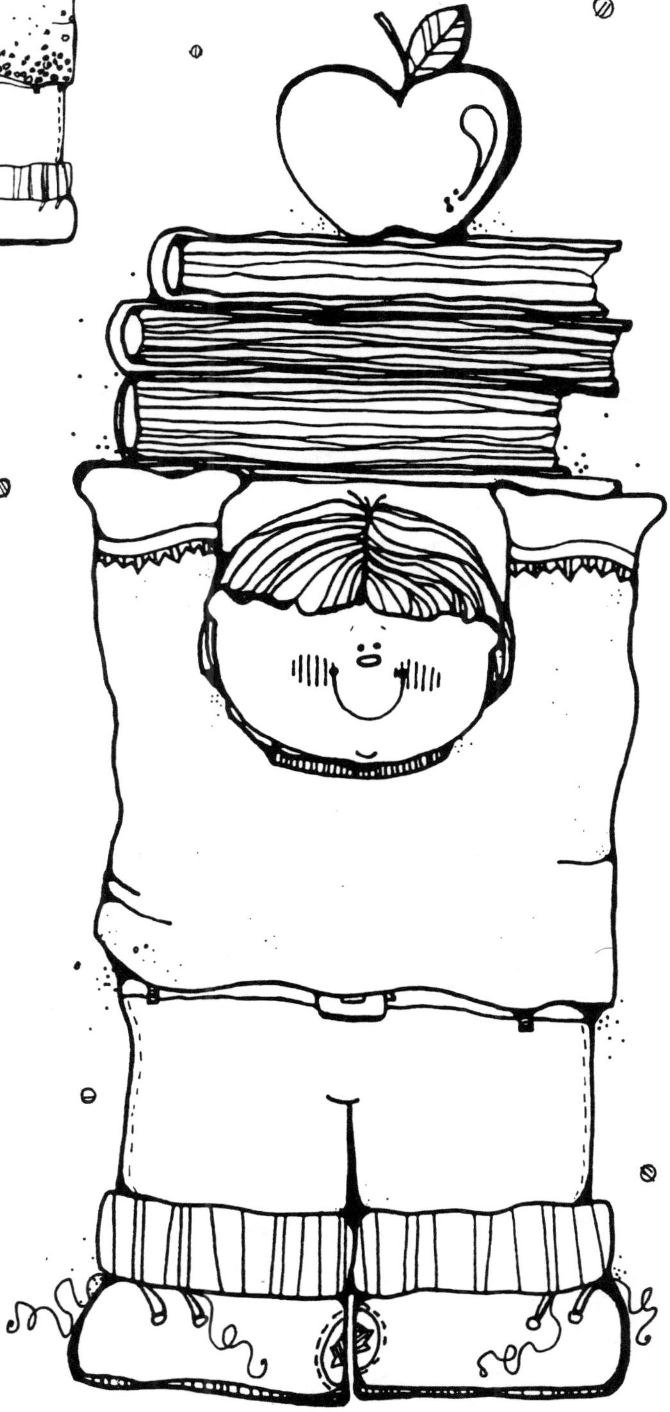

School Lunch!

field trip!

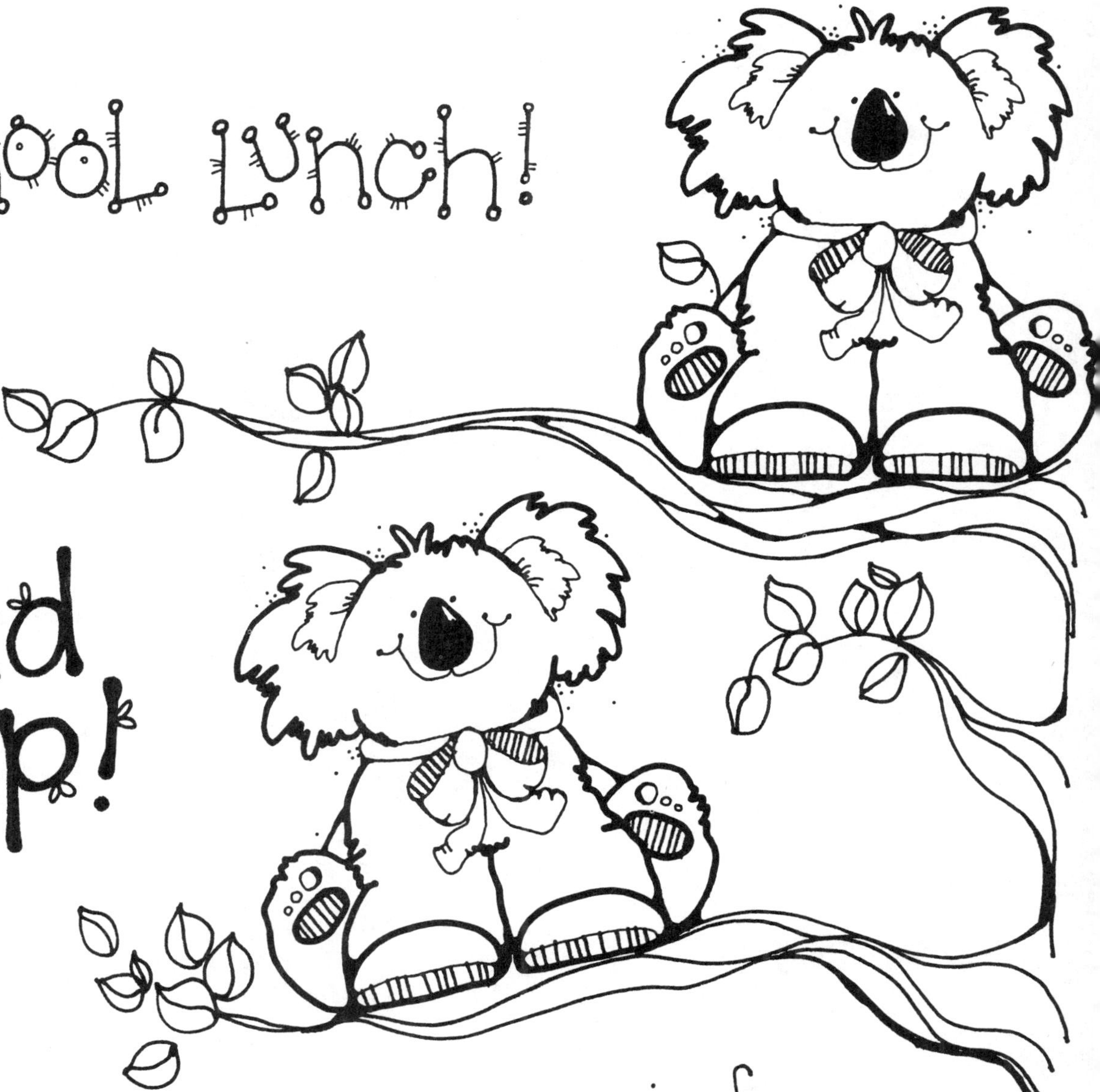

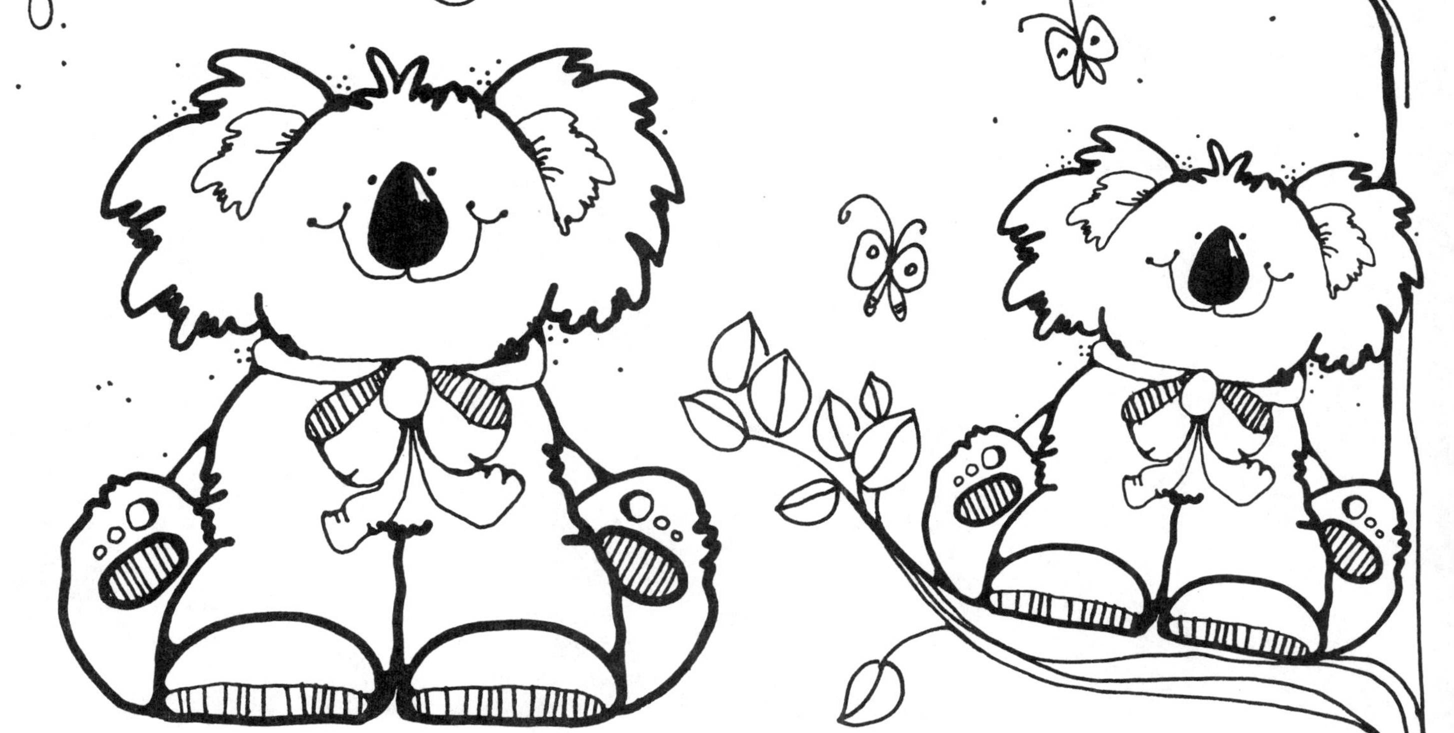

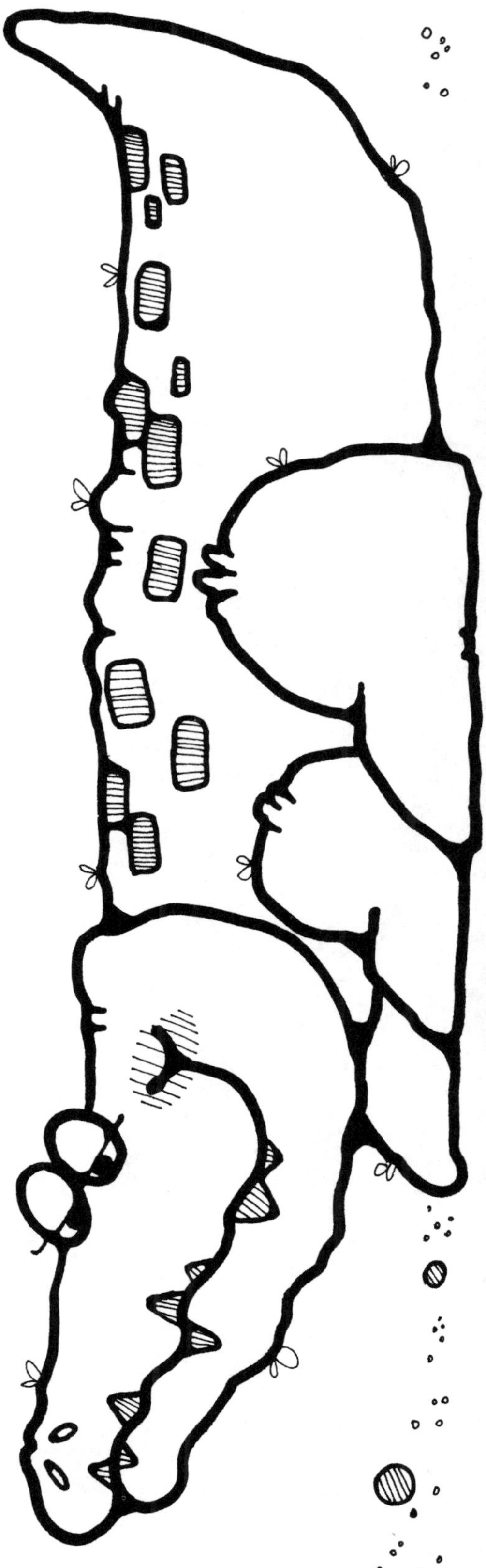

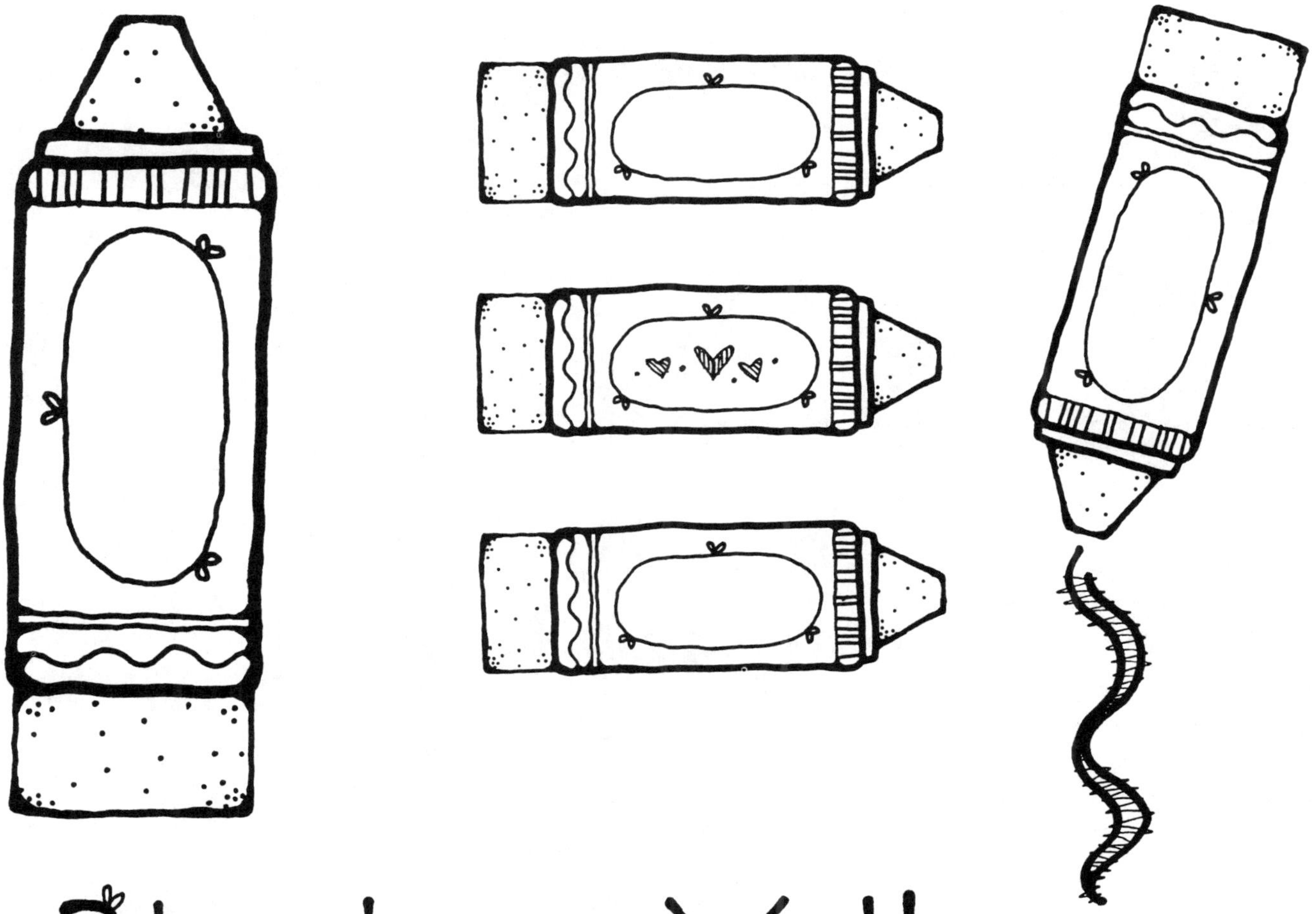

Black
White
Red
Blue

Yellow
Green
Brown
Orange

these are a few of my favorite things...

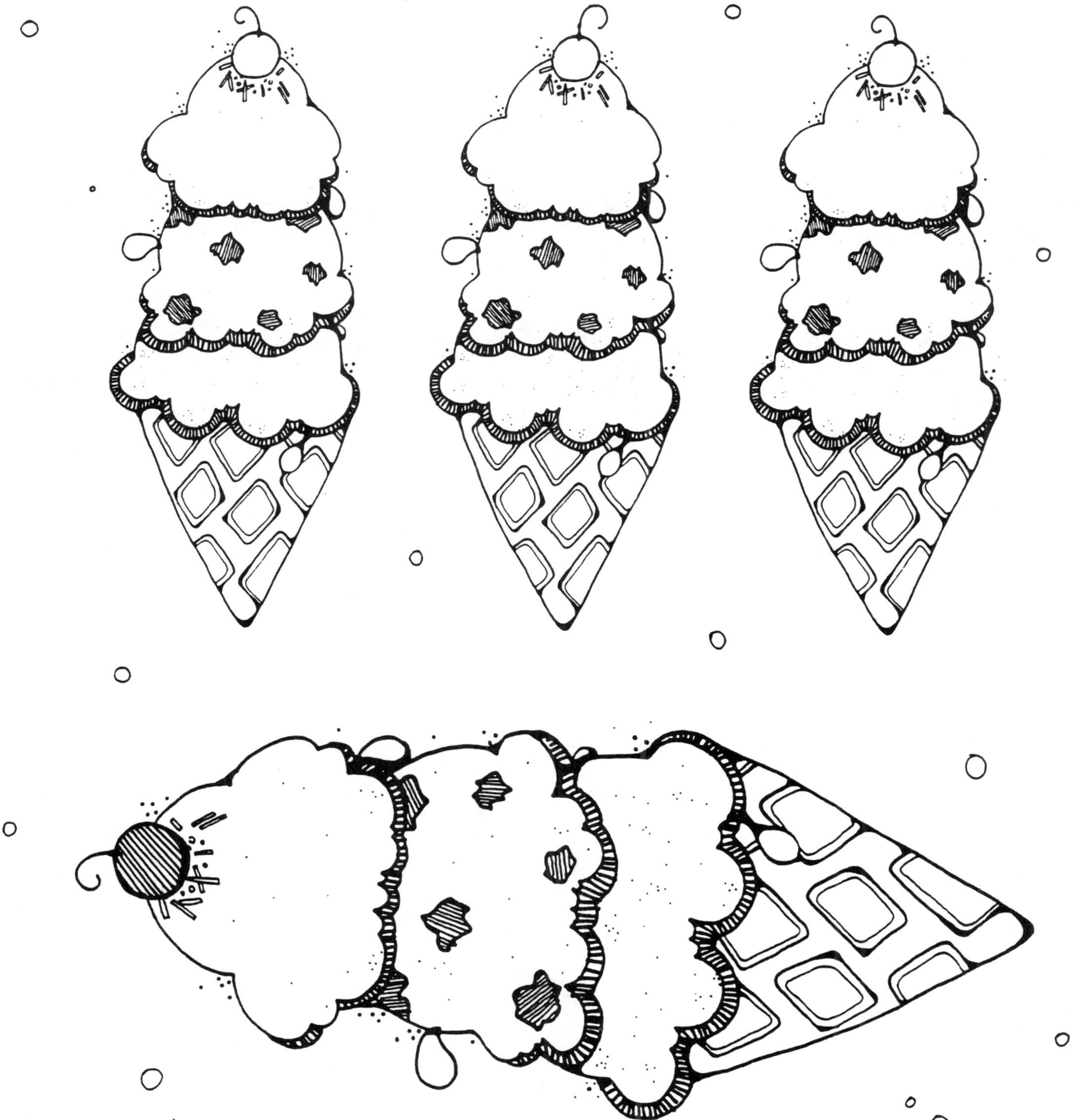

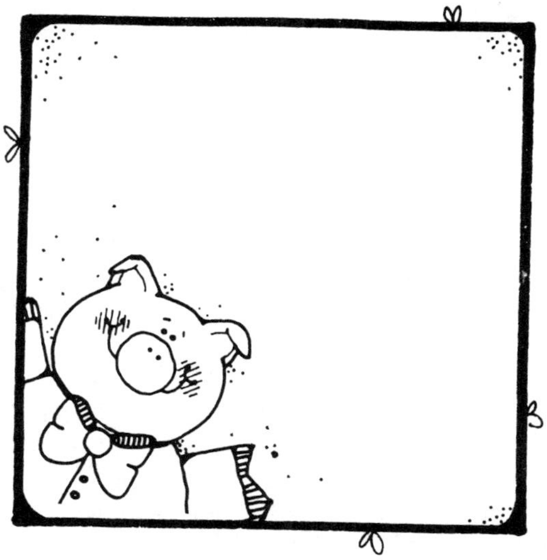

DON'T FORGET

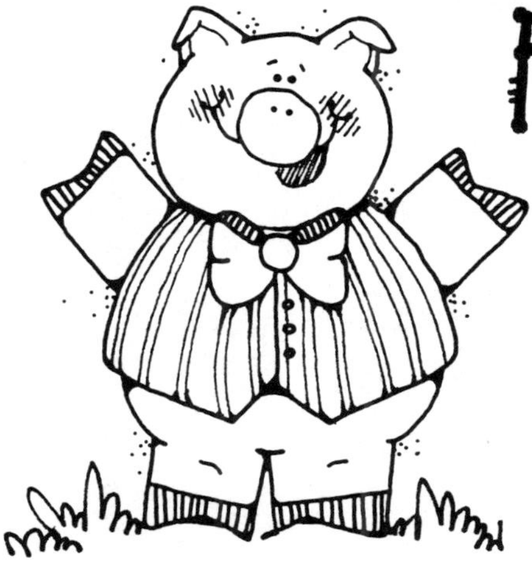

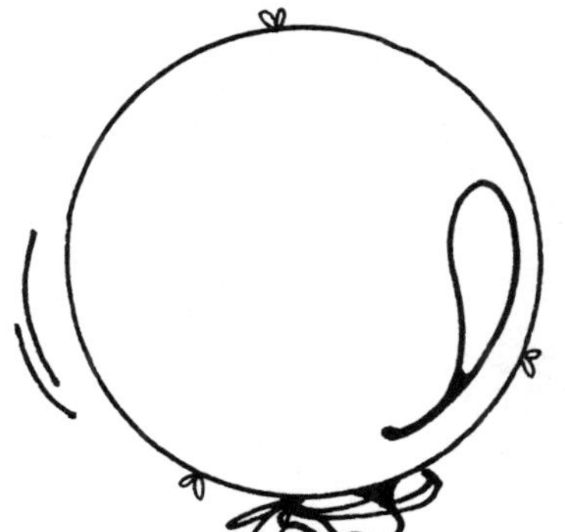

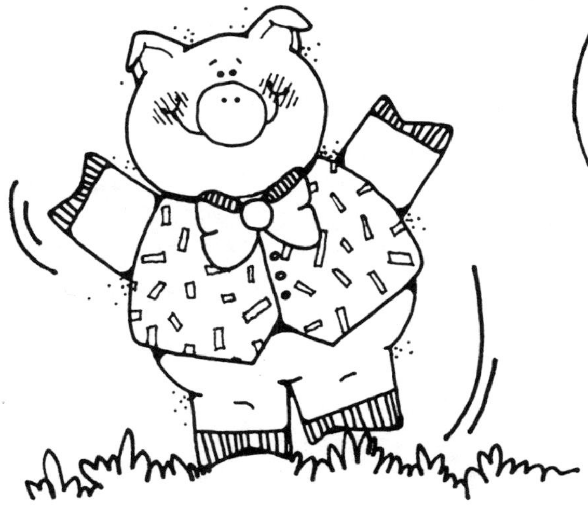

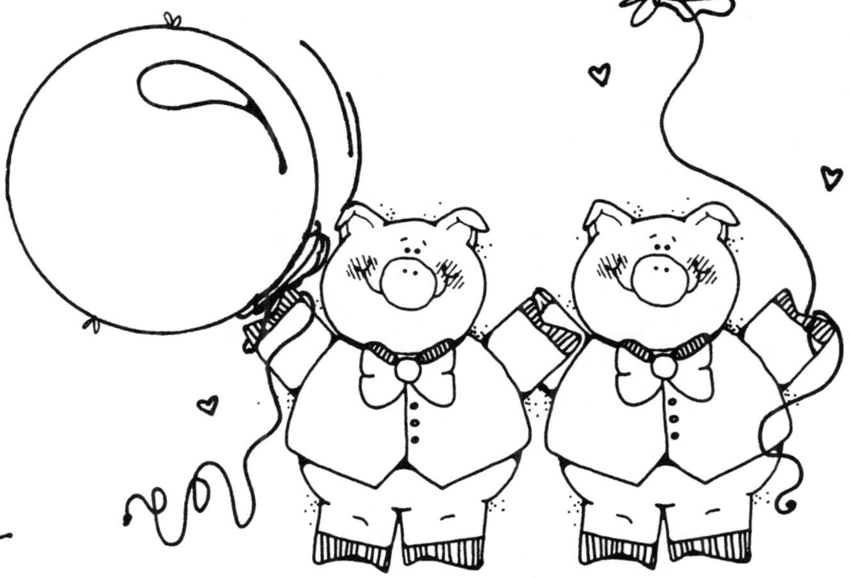

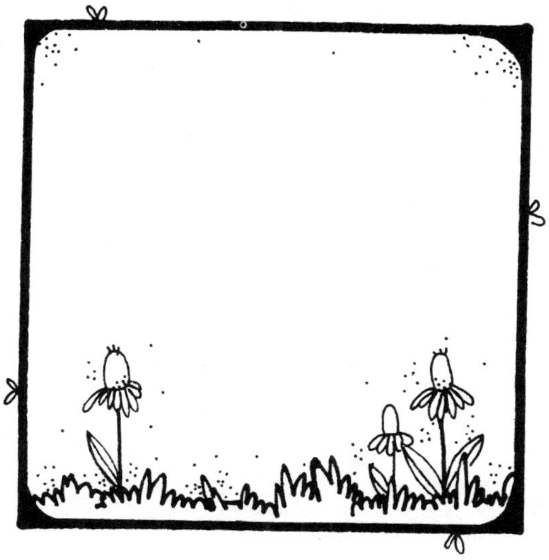

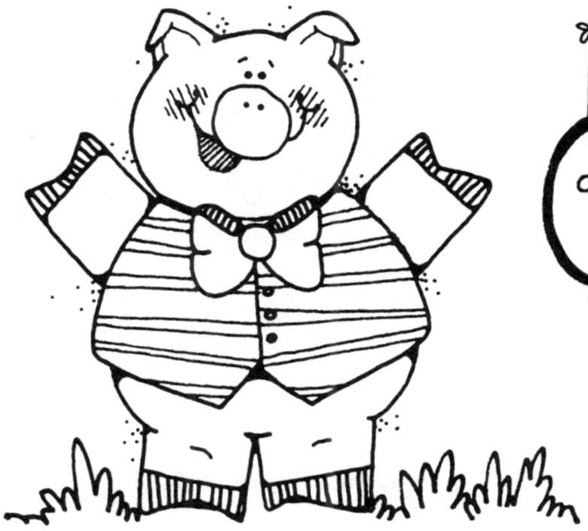

PIG OUT!

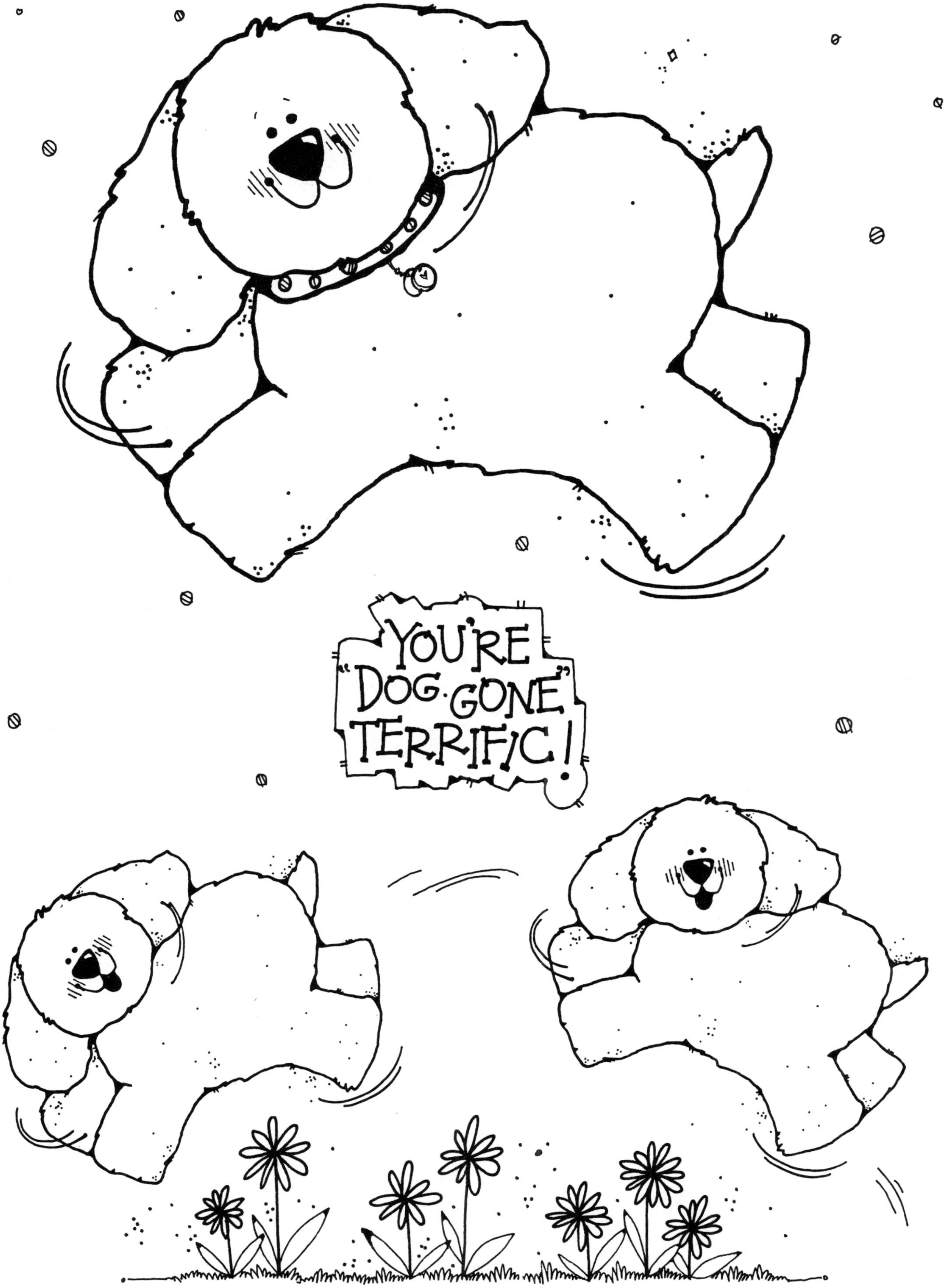
YOU'RE
"DOG·GONE"
TERRIFIC!

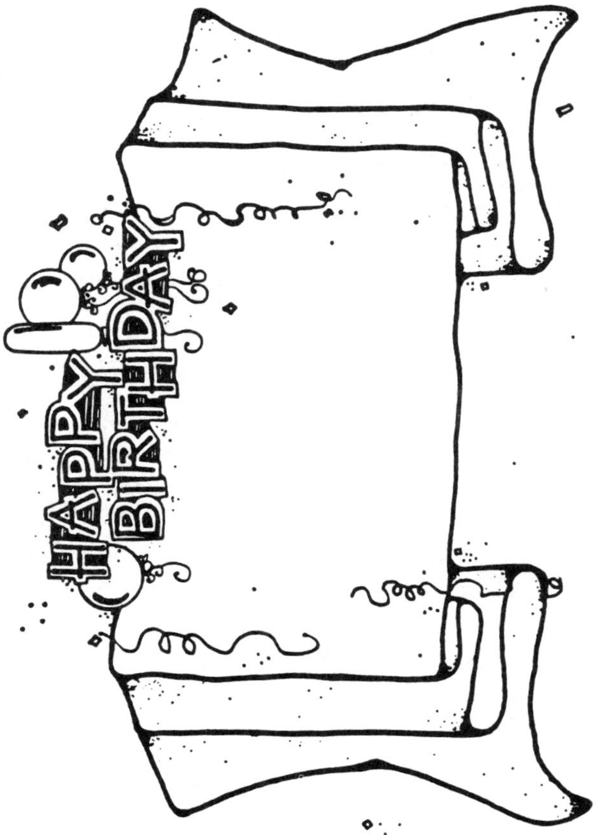
HAPPY BIRTHDAY

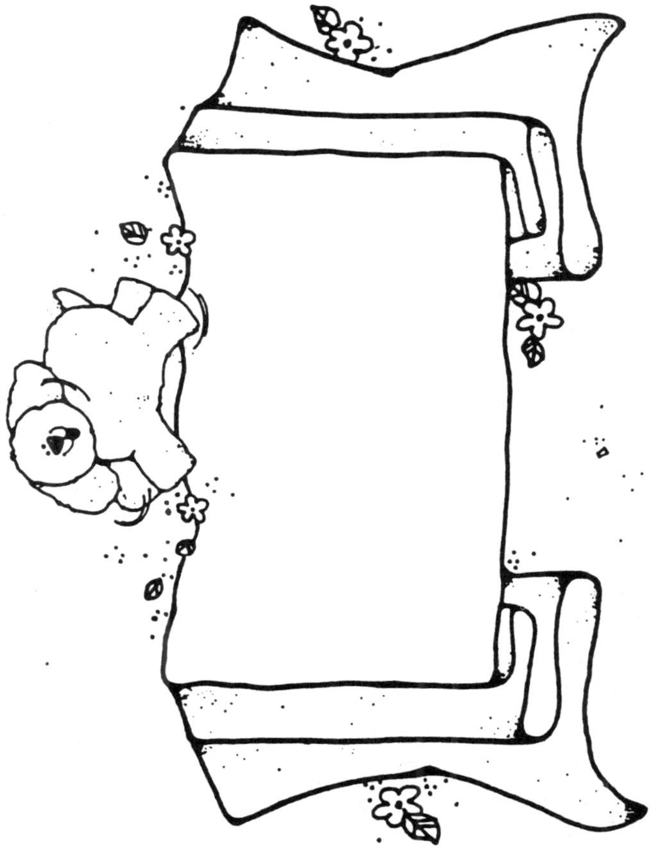

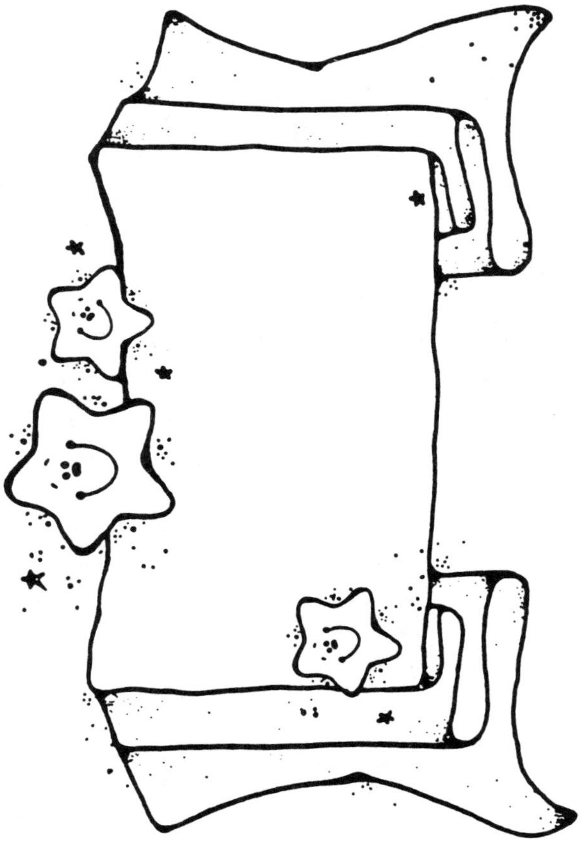

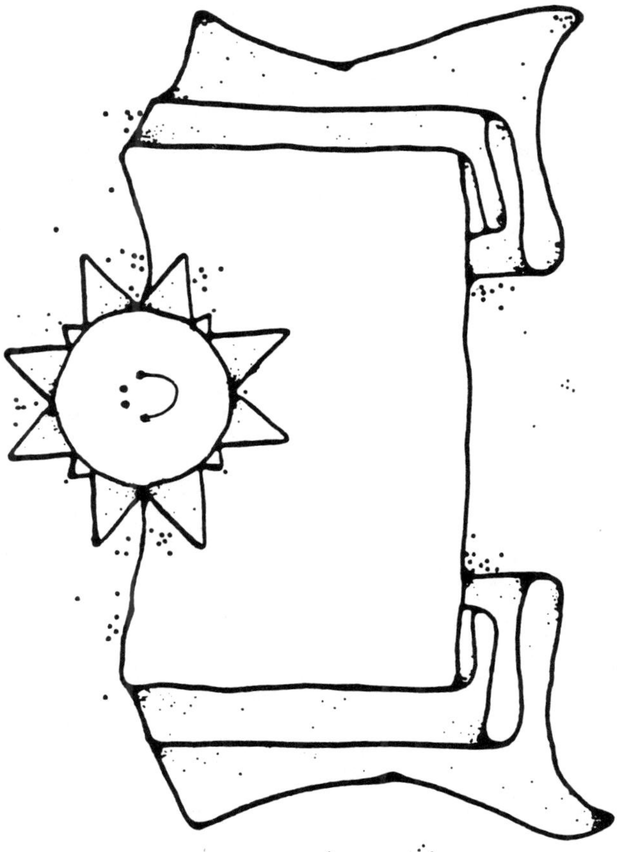

something to "ROAR" for...

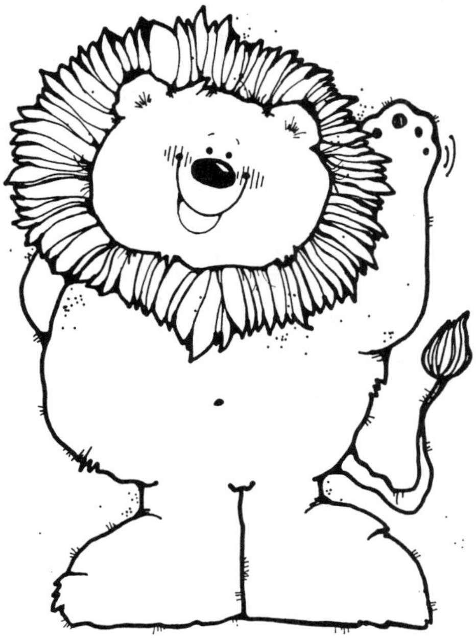

NO "LION"... YOURE THE BEST !!!

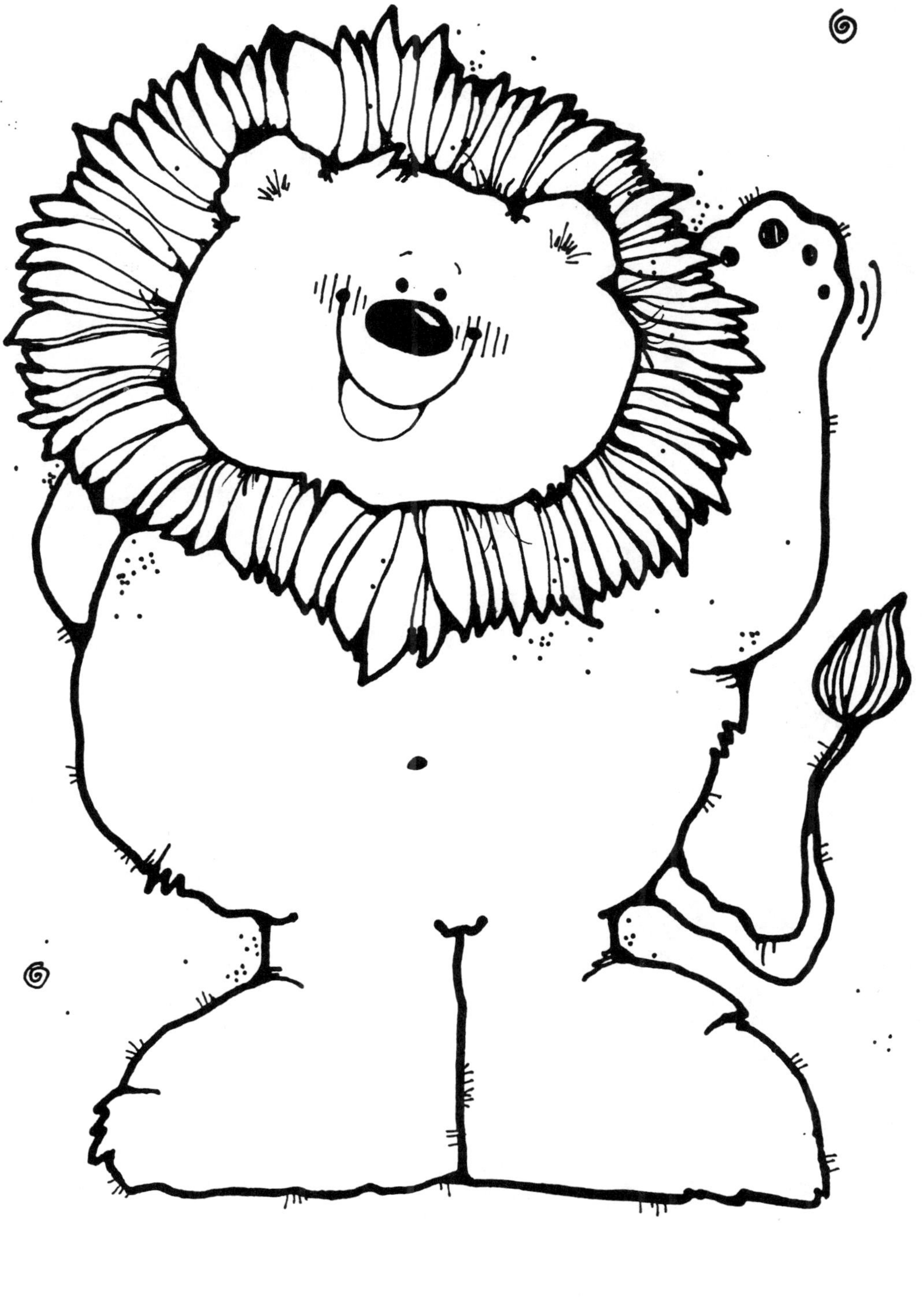

SOCCER PRACTICE

Little League

PAC MEETING

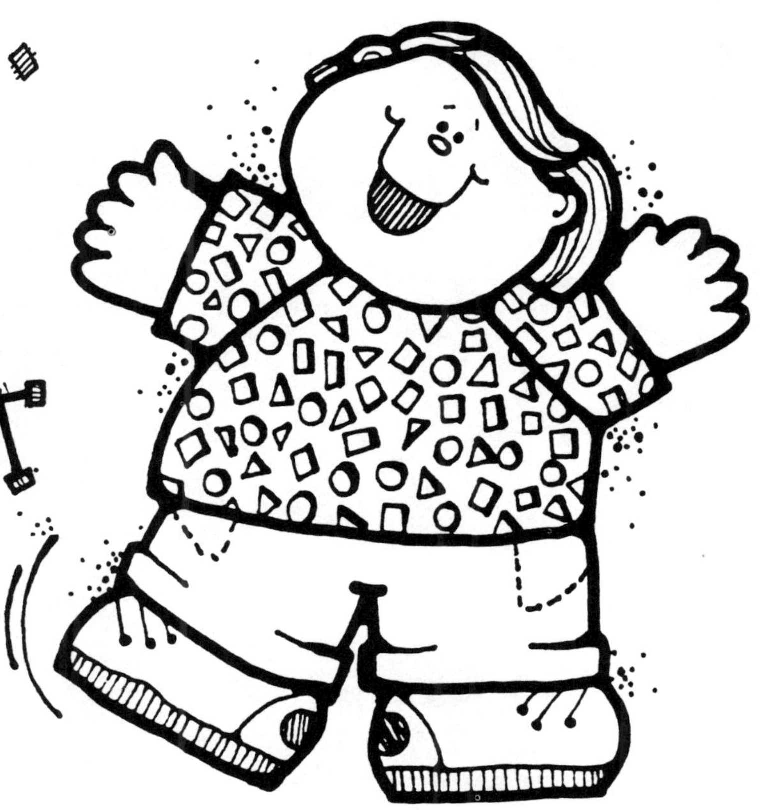

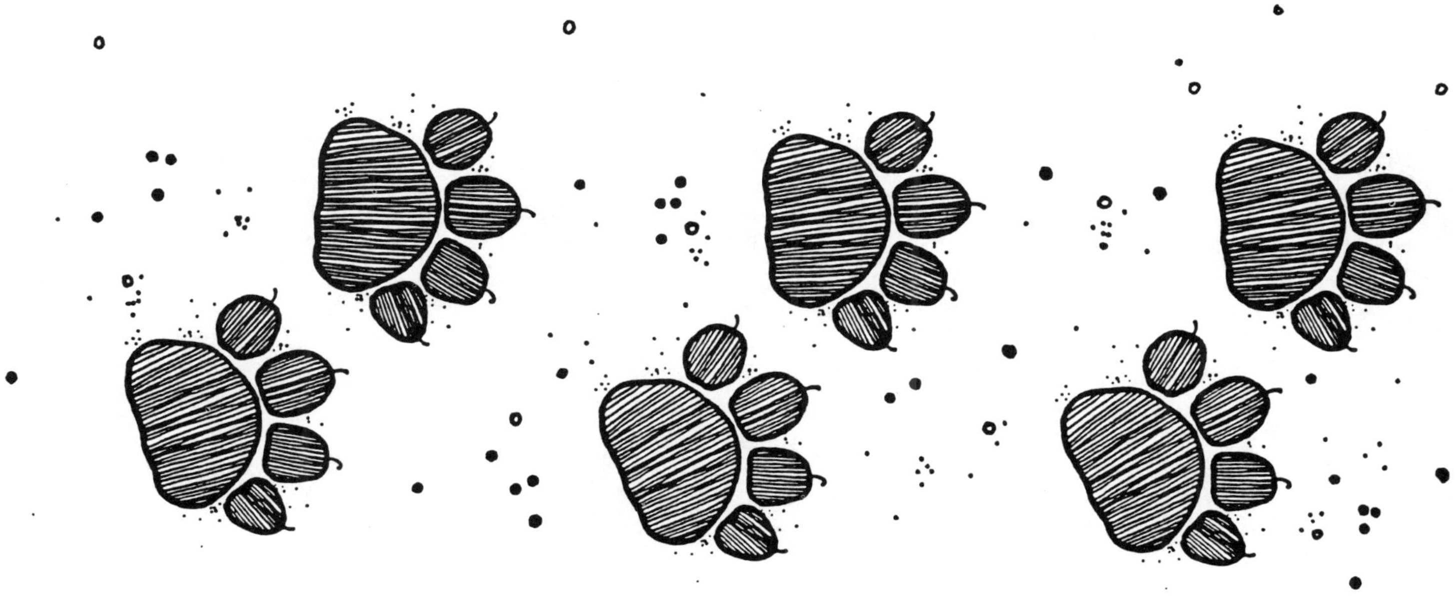

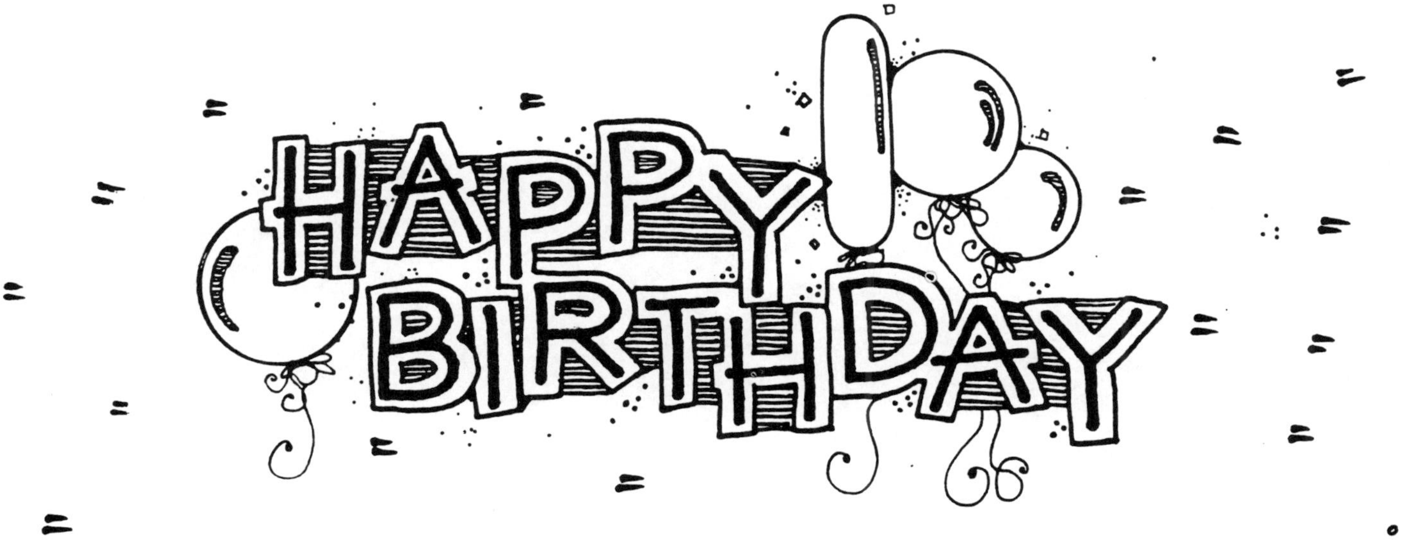
HAPPY
BIRTHDAY

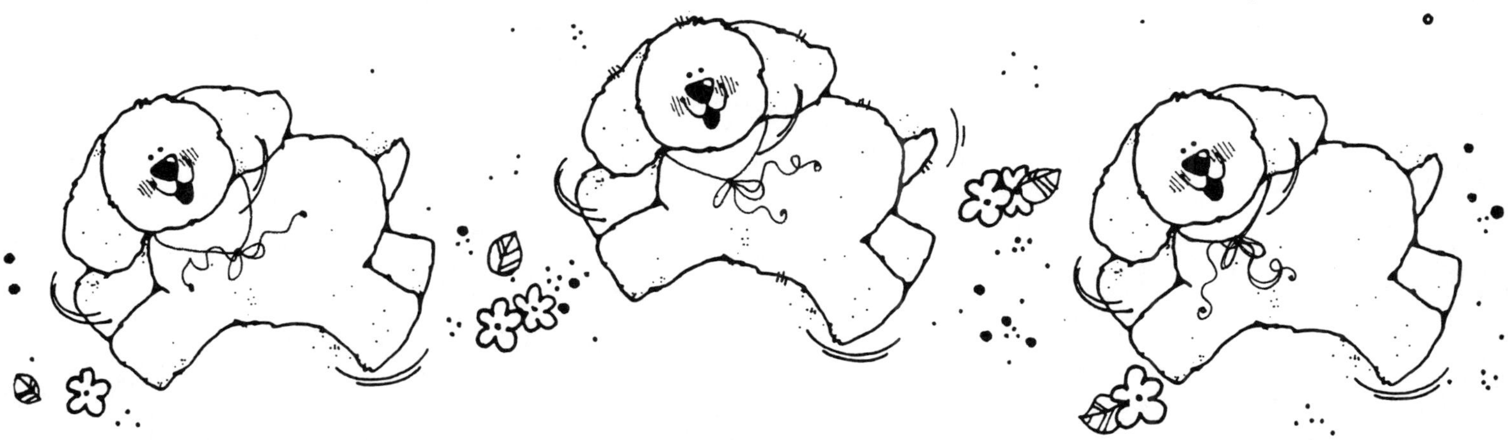

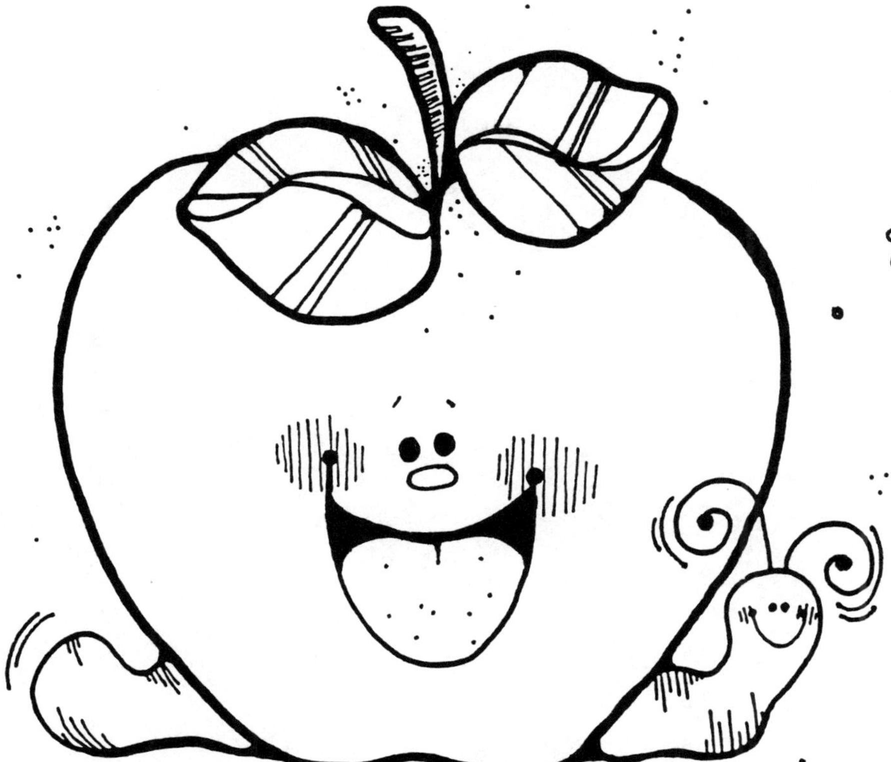

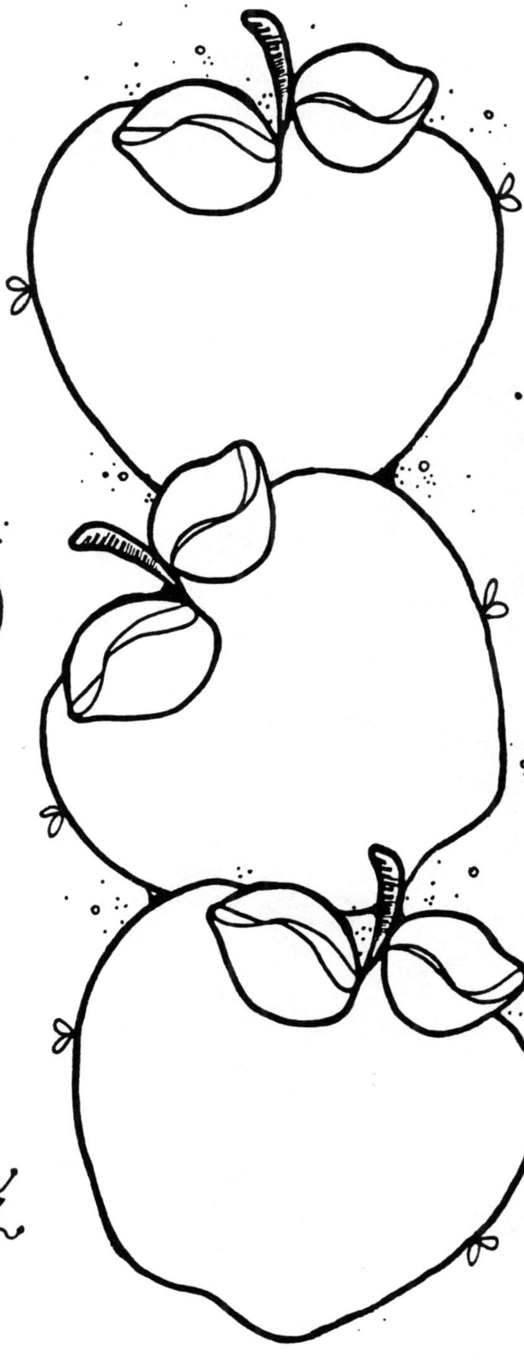

SCHOOL IS COOL

SCHOOL IS COOL

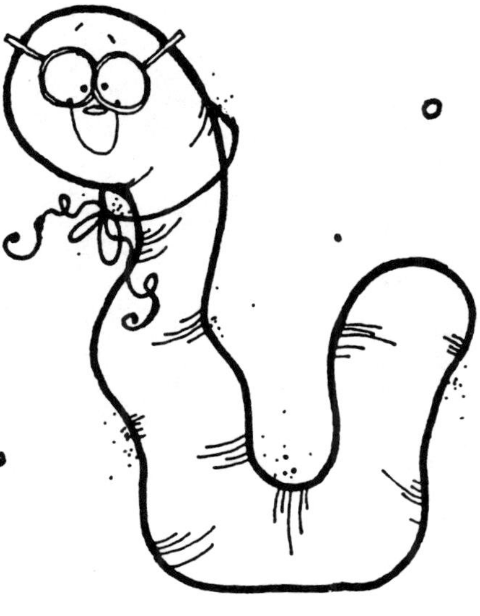

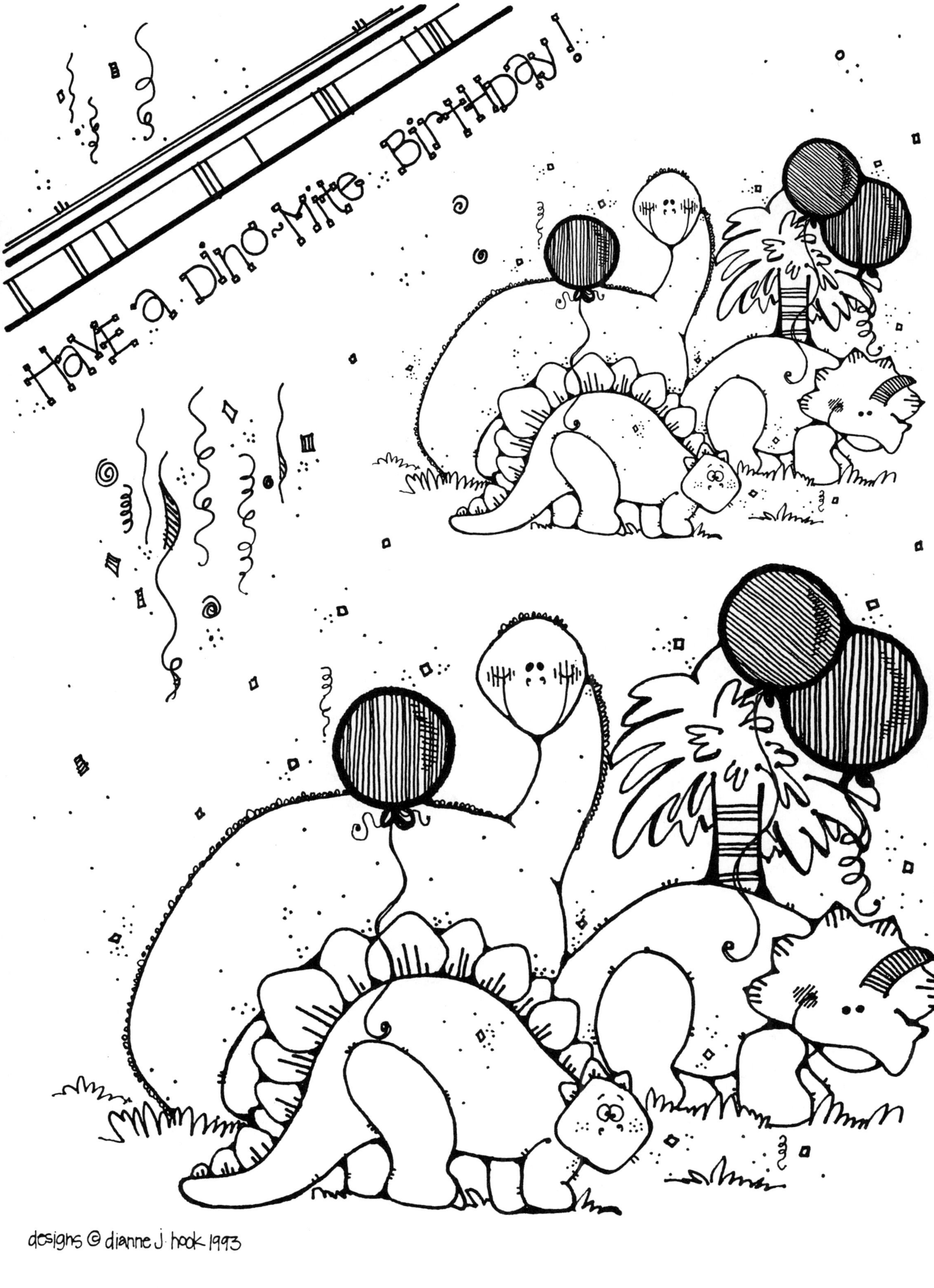
Have a Dino-Mite Birthday!

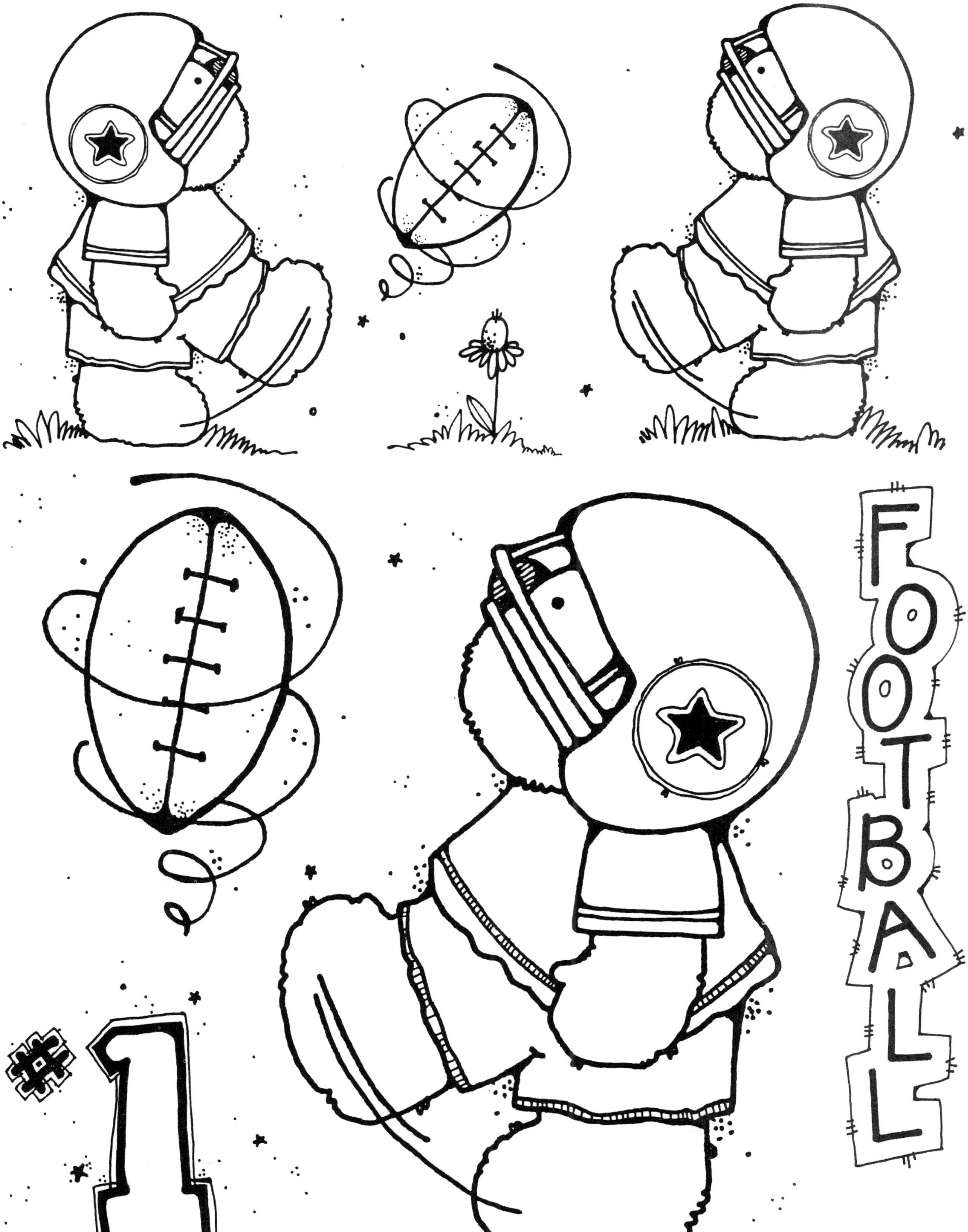
#1
FOOTBALL

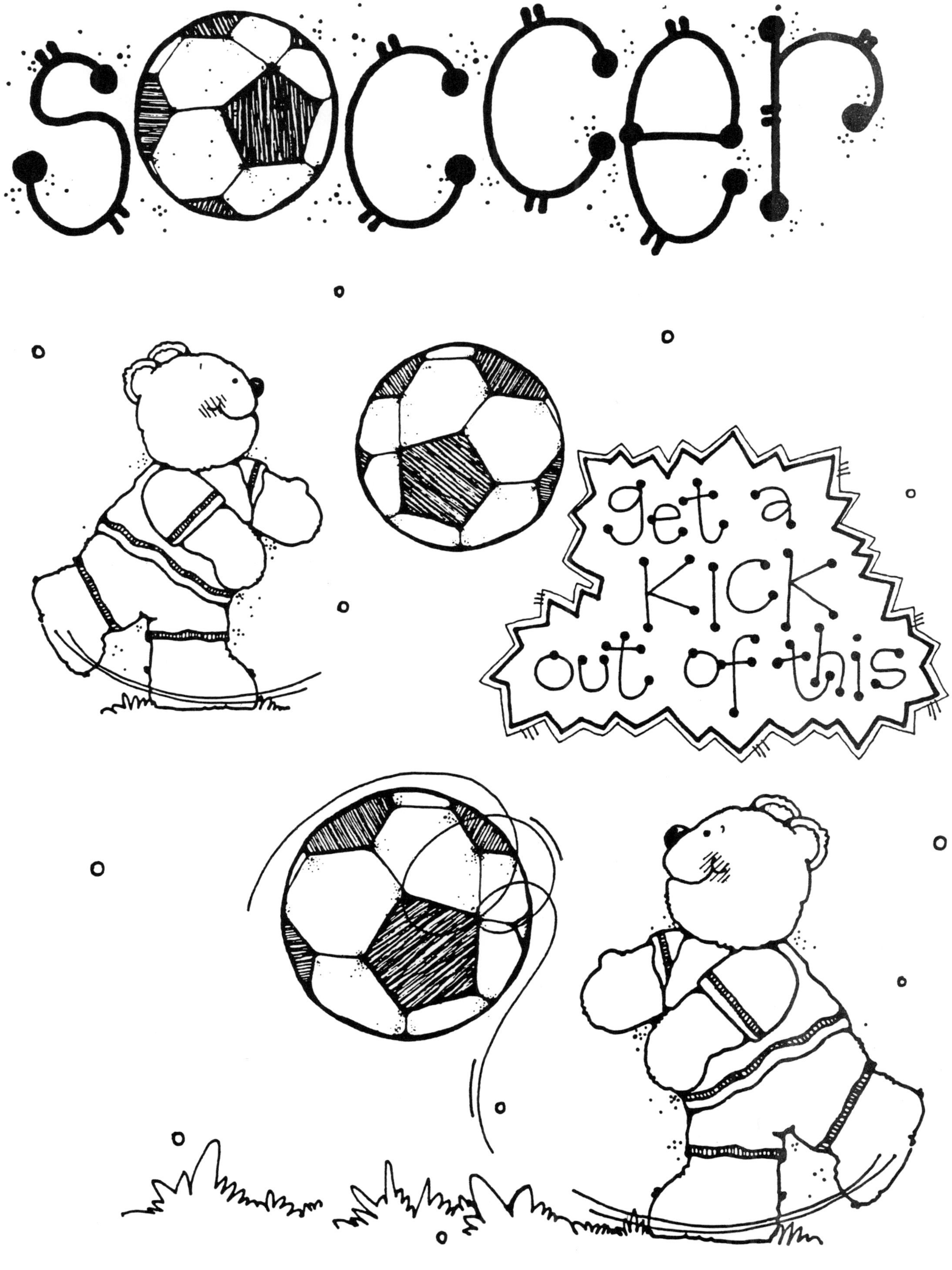
soccer
get a KICK out of this

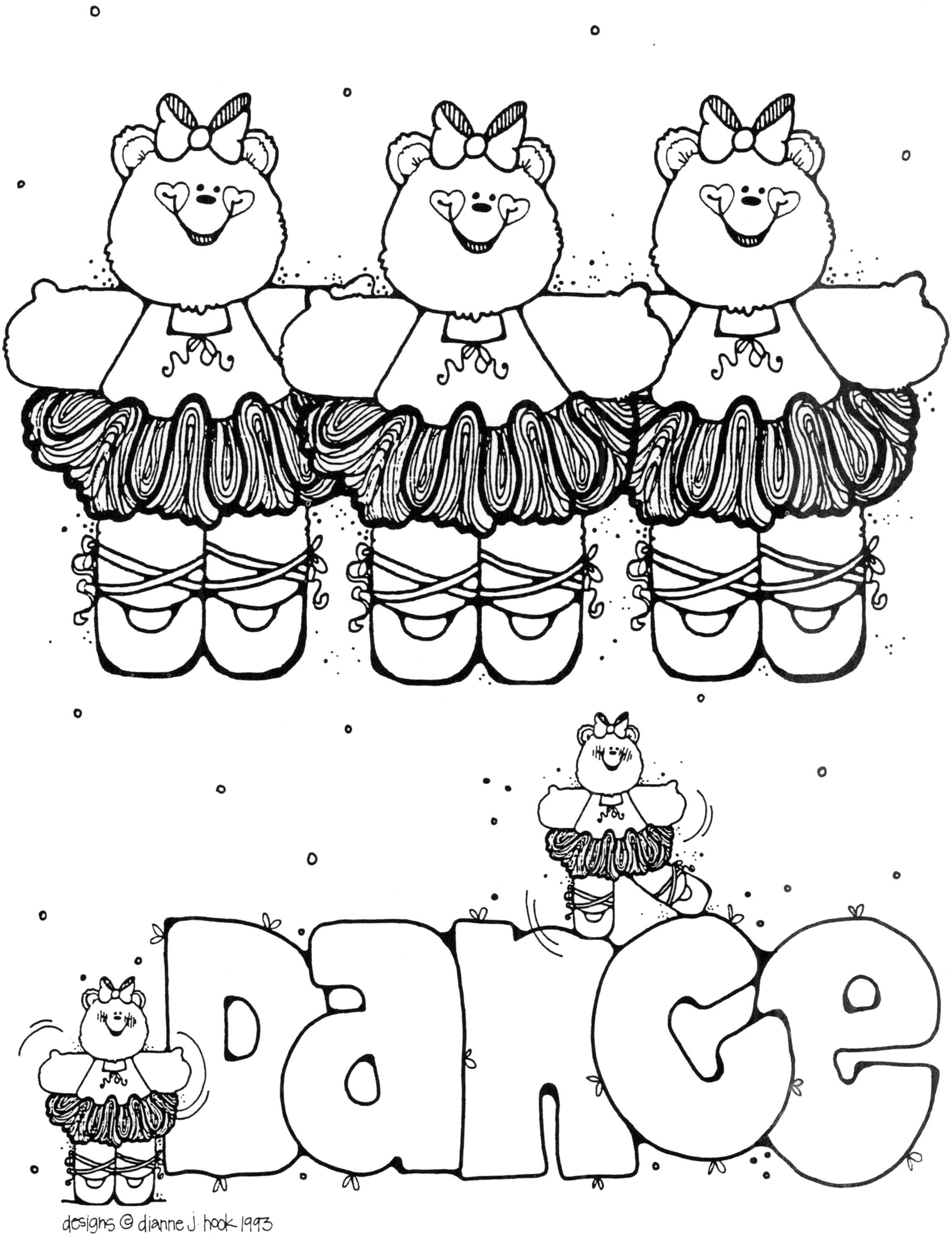
Dance
designs © dianne J. hook 1993

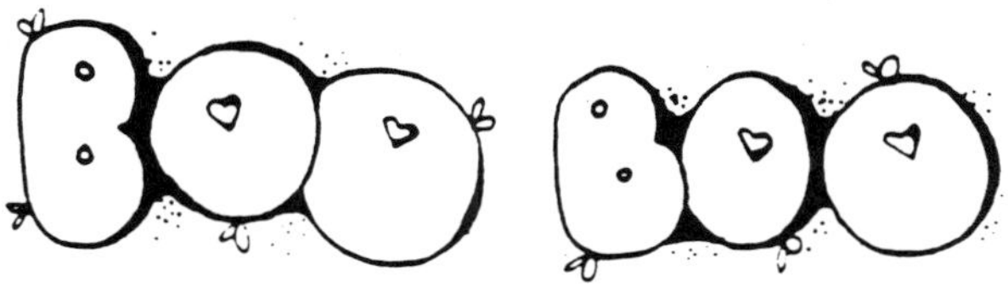
BOO BOO

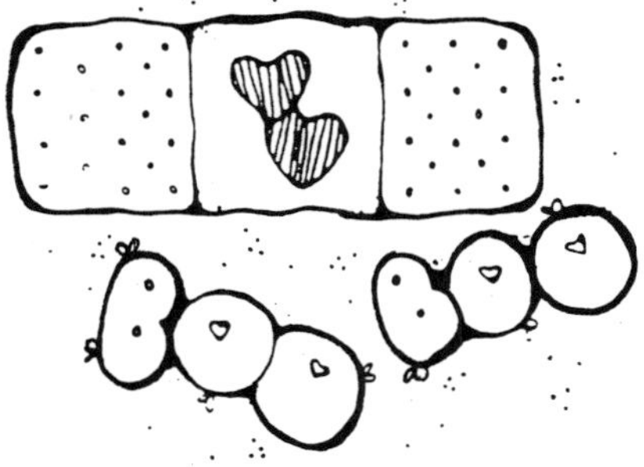
BOO BOO

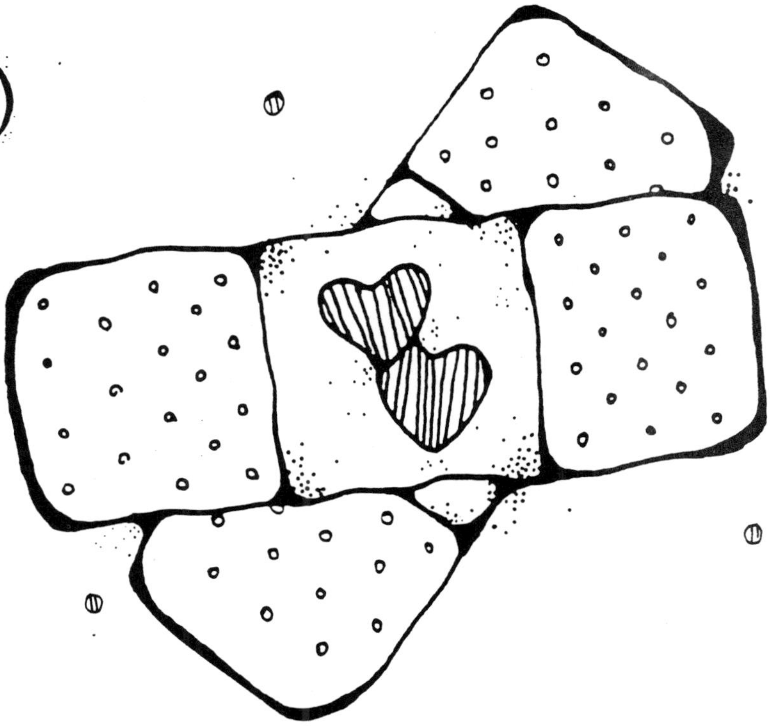

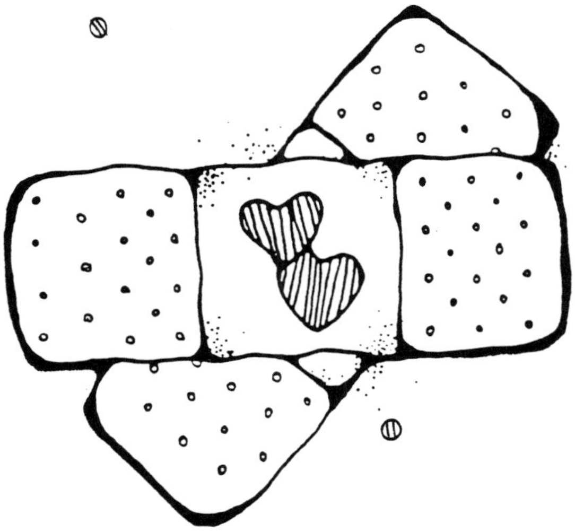

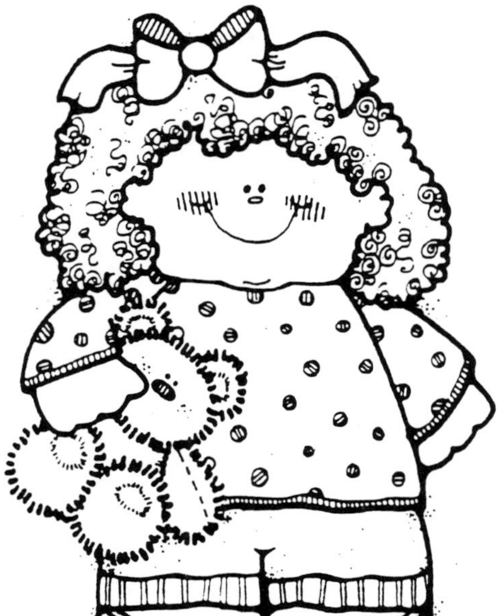

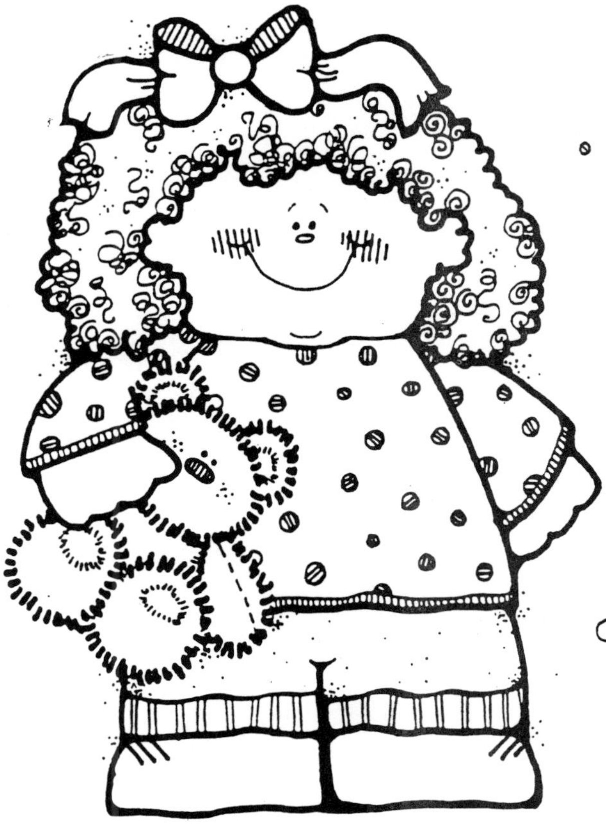